Ian Kirby

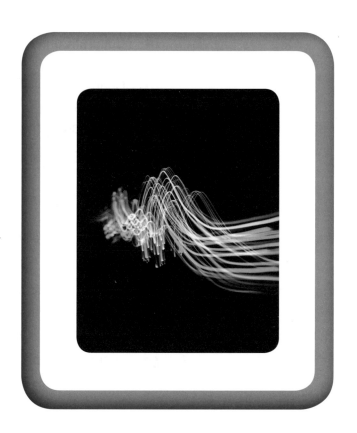

ESSENTIALS

GCSE AQA

English Literature

Contents

What to Expect in the Exam

In **Unit 1**, **Section A** of the exam, you'll be given a **choice of two questions** on the text that you've studied. You'll need to answer one of these questions in **45 minutes**; you should read the question carefully, then spend **3–5 minutes planning** your ideas before you begin writing.

This **question** is worth 20% of your final GCSE mark.

If you've studied the short stories from the *Sunlight on the Grass* anthology, you'll still get a choice of **two questions** but they'll be in **two parts**:
- **Part (a)** will ask you about an aspect of a specific story.
- **Part (b)** will ask you to explore how the same aspect appears in another story of your choice from the anthology.

How the Exam is Assessed

In this part of the exam, you're being examined on the following assessment objectives:

AO1	Respond to texts critically and imaginatively; select and evaluate relevant textual detail to illustrate and support interpretations.	50% of this question
AO2	Explain how language, structure and form contribute to writers' presentation of ideas, themes and settings.	50% of this question

Spelling, Punctuation and Grammar

There will be up to **four marks** awarded for the accuracy of your writing. When writing your answers, it's important to consider:
- **Spelling**: you'll be expected to be able to spell familiar words, key words and names linked to your text.
- **Punctuation**: full stops must be used accurately, commas should separate parts of sentences, and quotation marks need go before and after quotations.
- **Grammar**: remember to use capital letters correctly, don't confuse your tenses and avoid mistakes with homonyms (words that sound the same but have a different meaning and are spelled differently).

Use the information on page 81 to avoid common mistakes in your writing.

Understanding Your Text

Whichever modern prose or drama text you're studying, you'll need to have a good understanding of:
- **Characters**: who the main characters are, how they act and why.
- **Setting**: where and when the text is set, and its effect on the characters and their lives.
- **Themes**: how ideas and issues are explored in the story and portrayed to the reader.

- **Language, structure and form**: how the writer uses these techniques to convey meaning.

For drama texts, it's important to remember that it was written to be performed. You should think about how the ways the play is performed can help to convey meaning.

1A Modern Prose or Drama: Character

The Main Characters

Questions in the exam can ask about a character in the text you've studied. It's important you are able to identify who the **main characters** (sometimes called **protagonists**) are. Examples of main characters include:

Prose	Main Characters	Drama	Main Characters
My Polish Teacher's Tie (from the *Sunlight on the Grass* anthology)	Carla, Steve, Valerie	*Under Milk Wood*	The narrator, Captain Cat, Reverend Jenkins
Lord of the Flies	Ralph, Piggy, Jack	*The Crucible*	John Proctor, Elizabeth Proctor, Abigail, Reverend Hale
Martyn Pig	Martyn, Alex, William, Aunty Jean	*Kindertransport*	Eva / Evelyn, Lil, Faith, Helga
Touching the Void	Joe Simpson, Simon Yates	*An Inspector Calls*	Inspector Goole, Arthur Birling, Sybil, Sheila, Eric
The Woman in Black	Arthur Kipps, Mr Daily, Mr Jerome	*Deoxyribonucleic Acid (DNA)*	Lea, Phil, Brian, Mark

What the Main Characters Are Like

You need to know what the main characters are like and how they are portrayed (in other words, their **characterisation**).

To work out what characters are like, look at:
- Their actions
- What they say
- What other characters say about them
- Their relationships
- How the writer uses language to portray them.

For example:
- Martyn is naive, thoughtful and in love, but has a miserable life.
- Joe Simpson is adventurous, brave, skilful and rational.
- Captain Cat is dissatisfied and tormented; he feels trapped and sad.
- Faith is independent and loving, but insecure and lonely.

You should also think about the character's **age**, **gender**, **social class**, **physical appearance**, **personality traits**, **attitudes and opinions**.

Proving Your Ideas with Quotations

Once you've worked out what each of the characters is like, you need to be able to **prove your ideas**. The best way to do this is by using quotations. For example:
- Martyn has a miserable life, 'Did I hate him? He was a drunken slob and he treated me like dirt. What do you think? Of course I hated him.'
- Joe is rational, 'I was injured and unlikely to survive. Simon could get down alone. [...] I remained silent, but it was no longer for fear of losing control. I felt coldly rational.'

- Captain Cat is tormented, 'Like a cat, he sees in the dark. Through the voyages of his tears, he sails to see the dead.'
- Faith is insecure, 'I have never been a good enough daughter. [...] I've always thought it was my fault that you were so unhappy.'

The quotations don't have to be things the characters say; they can be things that are said about them by other characters.

Analysing Your Quotations

You also need to be able to comment on the **effect of specific words** in your quotations. Use the **PEA technique (Point, Evidence, Analysis)**, also known as the 'PEE technique' (Point, Evidence, Explanation), the 'PEC technique' (Point, Evidence, Comment) or the '1 2 3 technique'. The following student responses are structured using PEA:

State your point, or idea, about the character

⬇

Support your point with evidence

⬇

Analyse how techniques of language, structure or form help to show what the character is like

Develop your analysis further

Martyn Pig

Martyn has a miserable life, 'Did I hate him? He was a drunken slob and he treated me like dirt. What do you think? Of course I hated him.' The simile shows us that Martyn's home life is bad; the adjectival phrase 'drunken slob', and the use of the question and answer highlight the poor relationship with his father.

Touching the Void

Joe is rational, 'I was injured and unlikely to survive. Simon could get down alone. [...] I remained silent, but it was no longer for fear of losing control. I felt coldly rational.' The use of short sentences and the matter-of-fact tone, suggest Joe accepts the terrible situation. This is emphasised by the adverbial phrase at the end, suggesting a lack of emotion.

Under Milk Wood

Captain Cat is tormented, 'Like a cat, he sees in the dark. Through the voyages of his tears, he sails to see the dead.' The metaphors show the Captain's sadness and the way he is haunted by his dead shipmates. This is emphasised by the ironic simile that tells us that, even though he is blind, he cannot stop seeing the men every night and is never at rest.

Kindertransport

Faith is insecure, 'I have never been a good enough daughter. [...] I've always thought it was my fault that you were so unhappy.' The phrase 'good enough' displays low self-esteem, whilst 'my fault' shows guilt. The fact that these insecurities are deep-rooted is emphasised by the intensifiers 'never' and 'always'.

Quick Test

1. Write down four or five words to describe a main character in the text you're studying. Find a quotation to support these characteristics.
2. Who is the nastiest character in the text you're studying? What makes you think this?
3. Who is the weakest character in the text you're studying? What makes you think this?
4. Who do you think is the most important character in the text you're studying and why?

Key Words   Simile • Metaphor • Ironic • Intensifier

How Main Characters Change

You may be asked how a **character changes** and **develops** through the course of the story. Think about **how they change** and **what causes them to change**. Is the change a positive or negative one? For example:

- *Anil* (from the *Sunlight on the Grass* anthology)
  Anil is innocent, fearful and a dreamer. When he is sent away to be educated, we see growing awareness and the development of a conscience.

- *Lord of the Flies*
  Piggy changes from a figure of fun to a figure of wisdom and common sense.

- *Martyn Pig*
  Alex seems funny, attractive, ambitious, but dominated. However, she later reveals confidence and strength, and proves herself to be untrustworthy and selfish.

- *Touching the Void*
  Joe is ambitious and adventurous, although socially awkward. His personal strength is tested, as well as his maturity, as he is forced to face up to a terrible dilemma.

- *The Woman in Black*
  Arthur changes from a confident, eager young man, to being weak, terrified and exhausted.

- *Under Milk Wood*
  As we meet the Reverend Eli Jenkins more, we see that, as well as being religious, happy and satisfied, he is realistic and hopeful.

- *The Crucible*
  Hale begins the play believing in witches and the process for discovering them, but becomes disillusioned and speaks out against the Church.

- *Kindertransport*
  Helga is guilty and upset about sending Eva away, but is also brave and feels she has done the right thing. Later, she is angry and hurt at being rejected.

- *An Inspector Calls*
  Sheila is self-centred, attention-seeking, excitable and seems naive. However, she becomes guilty, rebellious, wiser and more responsible for her actions.

- *Deoxyribonucleic Acid* (*DNA*)
  Lea is insecure, misguided and relies upon Phil but is ignored by him. She begins to argue with Phil and gradually becomes more independent.

Remember to look at all the main characters in the text you're studying. Are there other characters that you think go through significant changes?

Connectives

Connectives of Comparison

To show the examiner that you understand a character is changing, you should **link your ideas** with **connectives** of **comparison**:

- However,
- This is different in…
- In contrast,
- This changes when…

Connectives of Time

In addition, you could use connectives of time to show that you're referring to a later point in the text:

- Later on,
- After this,
- In Act 3,
- Towards the end…

Connectives of Consequence

If the character has changed for a reason, you could also use connectives of consequence:

- Due to…
- Because…
- As a result of…
- This leads to…

Selecting and Analysing Quotations

To prove your point, it's important to find quotations that show what the character is like at the **start of the text**, and how they **change in the middle or by the end**. When selecting quotations, you should look at **descriptive passages** or **dramatic moments or episodes** where the character plays a key part in making **decisions, conflict or emotional turmoil**.

You should make **specific comments** on how the language used in your quotations illustrates changing characteristics.

Look at how this has been done in the following student response:

> Connective phrase to establish your first point

> Quotation providing evidence

> Connective phrase to introduce your next point and show character development

> Use of connective of time to introduce the final point

> Analysis of language techniques used in quotation

The Woman in Black

At the start of the novel, Arthur Kipps refers to himself as, 'a sturdy, commonsensical fellow, and I felt no uneasiness or apprehension whatsoever'. The adjective 'commonsensical' shows that he doesn't get carried away, whilst the adjective 'sturdy' suggests mental (and possibly physical) strength. The word 'whatsoever' shows Arthur's confidence and lack of fear.

However, by the middle of the novel, Arthur seems considerably weakened, 'Now I felt heavy and sick in my head, stale and tired and jangled too, my nerves and my imagination were all on edge'. The list form and repetition of 'and' build up all the negative ways in which Arthur's experiences have changed him. The metaphorical 'on edge' adds to the sense that Arthur is becoming more nervous and fearful.

Towards the end of the novel, Arthur is physically and mentally exhausted, 'I slept wretchedly, waking every hour or so out of turbulent nightmares, my entire body in a sweat of anxiety, and when I did not sleep I lay awake and tense'. The majority of the language (adjectives like 'turbulent', nouns like 'nightmare' and the adverb 'wretchedly') is negative and linked to stress or fear. The long sentence, full of commas, reflects his panic and lack of stability.

Quick Test

1. In the text you've studied, which character undergoes the biggest change?
2. Do the characters in the book that you've studied change for better or worse? Why do you think this?
3. What different things in the text cause people to change?
4. Are there any relationships between people that develop and change?

Key Words   Adjective • List • Repetition • Metaphor • Noun • Adverb

The Importance of Setting

The setting and context of a text is important and often links with a story's themes and ideas.
To identify the setting you need to look at:

- **Time**: What time of day or year is the text set? Is it set in the present, past or future?
- **Location**: Is it set in an urban or rural location? What does it tell you about the society where the characters live?

Before you can analyse the effect of setting on the text that you've studied, you need to be aware of what the setting is. For example:

Prose	Setting
Something Old, Something New (from the Sunlight on the Grass anthology)	Edinburgh in Scotland, and Khartoum in Sudan, present day.
Lord of the Flies	A remote island, during an unspecified war (but with links to the 1950s).
Martyn Pig	An English seaside town, present day.
Touching the Void	Siula Grande in the Peruvian Andes, 1985.
The Woman in Black	Crythin Gifford, a fictional market town on England's east coast, early 20th century.

Drama	Setting
Under Milk Wood	The imaginary village of Llareggub in Wales.
The Crucible	Salem, Massachusetts, America, 1692.
Kindertransport	Set in England and Germany, the play features different times between 1939 and 1979.
An Inspector Calls	The Birling family's comfortable home in Brumley (a fictional, industrial city in the North Midlands), in 1912.
Deoxyribonucleic Acid (DNA)	An unspecified street, field and wood, in the present day.

For the text that you've studied, think about anything that **links to the setting**. For example, in Kindertransport, moving the setting between England and Germany, and different times, highlights the idea of being evacuated and displaced (and the effect this could have on somebody).

Exploring the Setting

The setting can create a certain **atmosphere**, or can help you to understand what a character is like. For example:

- In Lord of the Flies, the jungle setting is presented as beautiful but dangerous. This shows the two sides of the boys' nature (innocent and wild). Castle Rock also reflects Jack's character, whist the jungle fires create an atmosphere of panic.
- In Touching the Void, the setting creates an atmosphere of isolation, desperation and hopelessness. The extreme environment also reflects the extreme situations and decisions that the men are faced with.

- In An Inspector Calls, the family home reflects the comfortable lifestyle of the Birlings (in **contrast** to the life story of Eva Smith). This relatively small setting also creates a claustrophobic atmosphere, which heightens the drama of the arguments, accusations and revelations.
- In The Crucible, the time in which the story is set is important in understanding the characters' religious beliefs, the treatment of children and slaves, and how the hysteria could take hold so easily.

Analysing the Setting

Language and structure are used in a text to establish the setting. This can also create atmosphere, reflect a character's background, or show a character's feelings. You'll need to be able to select and analyse quotations from the text that show these things. The following student response shows how quotations are used in an answer to a question about setting.

> The Woman in Black
>
> The setting of Eel Marsh House in 'The Woman in Black' creates a sinister atmosphere, whilst also highlighting how Arthur underestimates the danger, 'I looked up ahead and saw, as if rising out of the water itself, a tall, gaunt house of grey stone with a slate roof, [...] isolated, uncompromising but, also, I thought handsome'. Personification is used several times to make the house seem alive and threatening to the reader, but also to show that Arthur is not scared. The adjectives, 'gaunt' and 'grey' sound ghostly and ill, warning us of the dangers inside.
>
> The sinister atmosphere around the house is increased when Arthur discovers the old graveyard, 'No names or dates were now decipherable, and the whole place had a decayed and abandoned air. [...] the wind rose in a gust, and rustled through the grass.' As well as the obvious link to death, the adjectives that are used to describe the unreadable and forgotten graves create an atmosphere of mystery and isolation. The use of different senses (the feel and sound of the wind) also helps the reader to imagine the bleakness of the setting.

Opening point about the setting

Analysis of descriptive language used to describe the setting

Further quotation providing evidence about the setting

Evidence of how the main character feels about the setting

Comment on the use of descriptive language

Quick Test

1. Find and analyse quotations that are important in creating the setting of the text you've studied.
2. How does the setting of your text help to tell you things about characters?
3. How does the setting of your text link to events in the text you're studying?
4. How does the setting of your text help to create atmosphere?

1A Modern Prose or Drama: Themes

The Themes of the Text

A theme is an **idea** or **issue** that's explored in a story. Themes are important because they make up the message that the writer wants to convey to the reader. The writer wants the readers to consider the issues and perhaps to see them from a certain **point of view**.

In the exam, you may be asked how a theme is presented and developed, so you need to know what the themes are in the text you're studying. There are usually a number of themes in a text, and they can be about anything, for example:

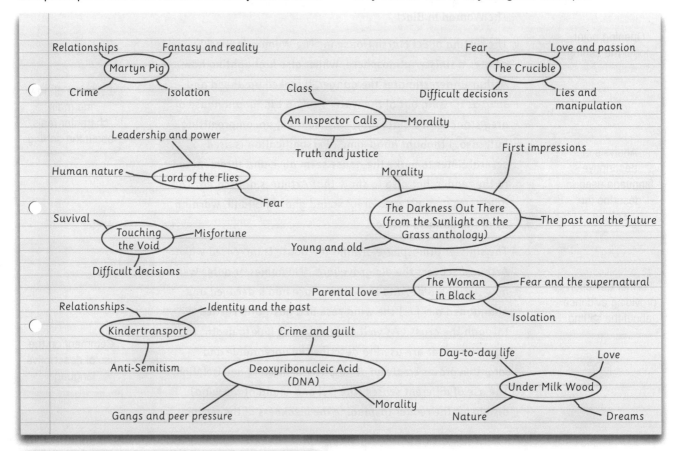

Where the Themes Appear

In order to **explore how a theme is developed** throughout the story, you need to know where it appears in your text. Themes can be explored through characters or events, for example:

* *The Crucible*
  Difficult decisions are made by Giles, Elizabeth and John. Despite pressure, they refuse to do things they see as morally wrong. In particular, John retracts his false confession and accepts his execution. This theme links to Miller's use of the play as an allegory of McCarthyism in the 1950s.

* *Martyn Pig*
  Fantasy and reality are explored through Martyn's love of murder mysteries, compared to his accidental killing of his father. His attraction to Alex also creates an **unreliable narrative**, with us eventually seeing what she is really like.

Think about how characters or events help to show the themes in the text you've studied.

Analysing How Quotations Illustrate a Theme

Once you know where the themes appear in your text, you need to look at how that theme is presented through the **author's choices of language and structure**.

Find quotations that show how a theme is presented and **analyse** them. You need to try to comment on what is being said about that theme, for example:

An Inspector Calls

Introductory point about the theme →

Quotation providing evidence about the theme ←

Mistreatment of the working classes is demonstrated by Mrs Birling. Sybil clearly believes that working class girls are of less worth than girls of a higher class, 'Girls of that class – [...] As if a girl of that sort would ever refuse money!'. The

Explanation of use of language →

repeated word 'that' is used to suggest distaste, as is the pejorative use of 'sort'. During the play, she is regularly given the word 'impertinent', to remind us that she doesn't like it if people present themselves as better than she is.

Development of the theme →

Her treatment of the working classes is seen as hypocritical because she is a member of the Brumley Women's Charity Organisation, and yet she admits, 'I wasn't satisfied with the girl's claim [...] and so I used my influence to have it refused'. The phrase 'used my influence' shows that she actually goes out of her way to not help Eva Smith.

This is emphasised by her summary of the events leading to Eva's suicide: 'I'm very sorry. But I think she only had herself to blame.' The dismissive tone of the second sentence, allows us to see the insincerity of the first sentence.

Quick Test

1. What do you think is the most important theme in the book you've studied? Why?
2. Which events in the text you've studied link to different themes? In what ways?
3. Which characters in the book you've studied link to different themes? In what ways?
4. In the text you've studied, are there any themes that cause conflict between characters?

Understanding the Question

In order to answer the question in the exam, first you need to understand it. Your question may read something like this:

> In *The Crucible*, how does the writer present the character of Elizabeth?

You need to **read the question carefully** and note the key words or phrases. For example:

- How and Present: The examiner doesn't want you to just describe the story. You're expected to **pick out quotations** and say how **specific words**, **punctuation** or **techniques** are being used to show things to the reader.
- Character: In the exam, you will usually get a question on a character (or a relationship between two characters) and a question on a theme. This will be the focus of your essay; **you shouldn't write about things that don't directly relate to the question** you've been given.

Making Your Plan

Before you begin writing your essay, you should **spend 3–5 minutes planning your ideas**. This could be as a **spider diagram**, **flow chart**, **list** or any other format that you're comfortable with. You could note down any **important page references** that you'll need when you come to use quotations.

When your plan is done, you should try to number it in a **logical order** so you write an essay that flows in a **clear** and **sensible** way.

The following plan is an example of how to approach the question above.

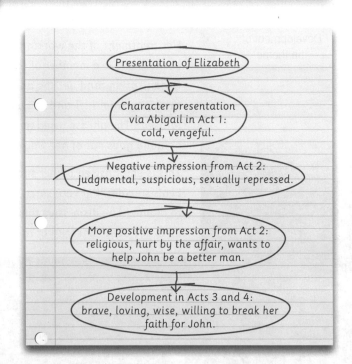

Answering the Question

When you begin writing, **follow your plan** and try to use a **clear structure**. It is important that you support your points with evidence and analysis using the **PEA technique (Point, Evidence, Analysis)**.

Choose your quotations carefully so that they *allow* you detailed analysis. If you choose a quotation without any interesting words, punctuation or

techniques, you'll find it hard to say anything about it.

If you've learned some quotations, that's great. It'll save you a lot of time as there'll be no need to search through the text. However, **only use quotations that you've learned if they're relevant to the essay title**.

What to Expect in the Exam

In **Unit 1, Section B** of the exam, you'll be given **one question** on the text that you've studied. You'll need to answer this question in **45 minutes**. It's separated into **two parts**:

- **Part (a)** asks you to respond to an extract from the text. You need to **quickly annotate the extract on the exam paper** in relation to the question set and then write your response.

- **Part (b)** asks you to explore the novel as a whole. You should spend **3–5 minutes planning** your ideas before you begin writing.

You must read the questions carefully so that you understand what it's asking of you.

This **question** is worth 20% of your final GCSE mark.

How the Exam is Assessed

In this part of the exam, you're being examined on the following assessment objectives:

AO1	Respond to texts critically and imaginatively; select and evaluate relevant textual detail to illustrate and support interpretations.	25% of this question
AO2	Explain how language, structure and form contribute to writers' presentation of ideas, themes and settings.	25% of this question
AO4	Relate texts to their social, cultural and historical contexts; explain how texts have been influential and significant to self and other readers in different contexts and at different times.	50% of this question

Spelling, Punctuation and Grammar

There will be up to **four marks** awarded for the accuracy of your writing. You should consider:

- **Spelling**: you will be expected to be able to spell familiar words, key words and names linked to your text.
- **Punctuation**: full stops must be used accurately, commas should separate parts of sentences, and quotation marks need go before and after quotations.
- **Grammar**: remember to use capital letters correctly, don't confuse your tenses, and avoid mistakes with homonyms (words that sound the same but have a different meaning and are spelled differently).

Use the information on page 81 to avoid common mistakes in your writing.

Understanding Your Text

Whichever text you're studying, you'll need to have a good understanding of:

- **Cultural context**: how the cultural background affects the story and its characters and themes.
- **Characters**: who the main characters are, how they act and why.

- **Setting**: where and when in the world the text is set and its effect on the characters and their lives.
- **Themes**: how ideas and issues are explored in the story and portrayed to the reader.
- **Language, structure and form**: how the writer uses these techniques to convey meaning.

Exploring Culture

As part of your study of literature, you will have read a novel that was written by someone living outside the United Kingdom. These texts are set in different parts of the world and present different cultures and ways of life. Culture refers to **somebody's** **background** and **sense of identity** and can be one of the main themes of the story. You need to think about how the **time, place, attitudes** and **beliefs** within the novel affect the story, its characters and your response as a reader.

Of Mice and Men

- *Of Mice and Men* was written by an American author, John Steinbeck, and published in 1937. The story is set in the state of California, during the Great Depression. At this time, many people lost their jobs, money was scarce and people travelled across the country looking for work.

- This context affects the story, as George and Lennie are two migrant workers. Steinbeck used his own experiences as a 'bindlestiff' in order to describe their lives. The two men's hopes are also linked to the Depression, and the idea of The American Dream.

- The context of early 20th century America also affects the characterisation of Curley's wife and Crooks in the novel. As a woman, Curley's wife is not seen as being as important as the men on the ranch. This is with the exception of Crooks who, as a black man, has even less social power. Although slavery had been abolished by the time the novel is set, equality of races did not exist and references are made in the novel to the practice of lynching.

Purple Hibiscus

- *Purple Hibiscus* was published by the Nigerian author, Chimamanda Ngozi Adichie, in 2003. The story is set in **post-colonial** Nigeria, at a time when the country had political and economic instability.

- Religion is an important part of the cultural context of the novel, with different forms of Catholicism being explored (one strict, one more liberal).

- The novel is set at a time of **gender** inequality, with men holding all the power (socially, economically and legally). The novel uses this in its exploration of how women and children are mistreated.

Mister Pip

- *Mister Pip*, by New Zealand author Lloyd Jones, was published in 2006. It's set on the island of Bougainville, during the civil war of the early 1990s. The ways a losing side are treated in a war lead to some horrible scenes towards the end of the novel.
- The religious and racial context is important in the novel. Mr Watts is unusual on the island because he is the only white man. This, along with her severe Christian values, causes Dolores not to trust Mr Watts and his influence on her daughter.

- Another aspect of the context is people's response to literature. The novel draws on the themes of *Great Expectations* by Charles Dickens, but it's more about the power of literature than one specific book. Despite being set in the 1990s, the village is isolated and we're told that there are no televisions or cinemas. This means that reading becomes much more of an escape for the characters of the book.

To Kill a Mockingbird

- *To Kill a Mockingbird* was written by the American author Harper Lee and published in 1960. The novel is set in the Deep South during the Great Depression of the 1930s.
- In the novel, we see different combinations of the three social prejudices of race, gender and **class**.
- At the time, despite slavery having been abolished, black people had fewer rights, lower earning power and less social status. The majority of white

people saw themselves as better, simply because of their colour, and lynchings were not unusual.
- Women had fewer rights than men, and their **domestic** role was clearly defined. This also meant that an abusive father or husband often went unchallenged. Scout can be seen as developing into an early **feminist**, and she is criticised by other characters for not fitting the more traditional image of a young girl.

Follow the Rabbit-Poof Fence

- Written by the Australian author Doris Pilkington, *Follow the Rabbit-Proof Fence* is based on a true story. Set in the early 20th century, it explores the 'Stolen Generation' of **indigenous** or Aboriginal Australians.
- Different chapters deal with Australia's modern history: the arrival of the English, the setting up of military bases and the first European settlers in the 1820s; the increased integration of

European settlers and Aborigines in the 1900s; the government's decision to remove mixed-race children from their families in the early 20th century.
- The novel explores the attitudes of different groups, black and white, to people of mixed race. We also see how Aborigines were feared or seen as worthless by some early settlers, as well as the importance of different **rituals**.

Quick Test

1. Can you find particular passages and quotations that link to the different contexts of the novel you've studied?
2. How does the context affect the thoughts and actions of the main characters in the book you've studied?
3. How does the context affect different events in the text you've studied?
4. How do you think the context affects your personal response to characters and events in the story?

1B Exploring Cultures: Character

The Main Characters

You must be able to identify who the **main characters** are in the text you're studying so that you can answer a question about them in the exam.

As the text you're studying is set in a different country, it's important that you think about how the **cultural background** affects the main characters.

You should consider:

- Their **religion** and **beliefs**
- The **traditions** in the society
- The **language** used.

First of all, you need to identify the main characters in the text you're studying, for example:

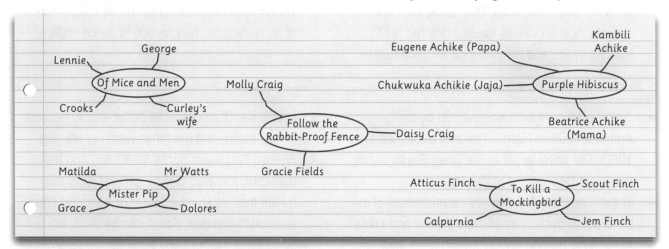

What the Main Characters Are Like

You may need to describe a character's **personality**, **appearance**, **background** and **relationships**.
For example:

- Curley's wife is dissatisfied, lonely, flirtatious and vindictive.
- Eugene is charitable and very religious, yet domineering and violent.

- Mr Watts is caring and committed but mysterious and an outsider.
- Calpurnia is maternal, firm, intelligent, and believes in respecting people equally.
- Molly is shy around new people but, with Daisy and Gracie, she is decisive, practical and a leader.

Proving Your Ideas with Quotations

In the exam, you need to make sure you back up your ideas using quotations, for example:

- Curley's wife is vindictive, 'Well, you keep your place then, Nigger. I could get you strung up on a tree so easy it ain't even funny.'
- Eugene is violent, 'my brother, Jaja, did not go to communion and Papa flung his heavy missal across the room and broke the figurines.'
- Mr Watts is caring, 'I will do my best. That's my promise to you children. I believe, with your

parents' help, we can make a difference to our lives.'
- Calpurnia believes in respecting people equally, 'Don't matter who they are. Anybody sets foot in this house's yo' comp'ny, and don't let me catch you remarkin' on their ways like you was so high and mighty!'
- Molly is a leader, 'Their big sister had proved herself to be a worthy leader. Her self control and courage, had never faltered throughout the trek.'

Analysing Your Quotations

The following student responses look at how the language or structure in a quotation shows things about character:

Of Mice and Men

Curley's wife is vindictive, 'Well, you keep your place then, Nigger. I could get you strung up on a tree so easy it ain't even funny.' The first sentence uses an order and derogatory language to create a threatening tone. This is then emphasised by her reference to the practice of lynching. The intensifier ('so easy') and colloquialism ('ain't') are also used to suggest that having power over Crooks is not difficult.

Purple Hibiscus

Eugene is violent, 'my brother, Jaja, did not go to communion and Papa flung his heavy missal across the room and broke the figurines.' The verb 'flung', coupled with the adjective 'heavy', show that Eugene can be violent and dangerous. The breaking of the figurines could be symbolic of how badly he treats his nice family.

Mister Pip

Mr Watts is caring, 'I will do my best. That's my promise to you children. I believe, with your parents' help, we can make a difference to our lives.' His speech is full of positive words: 'best', 'promise', 'difference'. These words, and his use of the second person ('you'/'our'), suggest investment in the children.

To Kill a Mockingbird

Calpurnia believes in respecting people equally, 'Don't matter who they are. Anybody sets foot in this house's yo' comp'ny, and don't let me catch you remarkin' on their ways like you was so high and mighty!' Her belief in respect is summed up in her first, short sentence. Her anger at Scout's social snobbery can be seen in the exclamation mark, the repetition of the imperative 'don't', and the simile she uses to criticise Scout's behaviour.

Follow the Rabbit-Proof Fence

Molly shows leadership, 'Their big sister had proved herself to be a worthy leader. Her self control and courage, had never faltered throughout the trek.' The adjectival phrase 'worthy leader' is emphasised by positive nouns ('self control and courage'). This is added to by the verbs ('proved', 'never faltered').

Make a point about a character

↓

Support your point with a quotation as evidence

↓

Analyse how the language or structure of your quotation shows what the character is like

Further analysis of your quotation

Quick Test

1. Who is the most interesting character in the text you're studying? Why?
2. Which character do you feel most sorry for? Why do you feel sorry for them?
3. Who do you think is the nicest or the most dislikeable? What makes you think this?
4. Who do you think is the most important, despite not being a 'main', character?

1B Exploring Cultures: Character Development

How Main Characters Change

It's important to know how characters develop and change in the text you're studying. You should consider the **influence of culture** on the character's development and relationships with other characters. For example:

- *Of Mice and Men*
  George is hopeful, kind and strict, but eventually loses his dreams and has to kill his best friend.
- *Purple Hibiscus*
  Jaja is intelligent and loving, but dominated by his father; he becomes more rebellious and is later hardened by his time in prison.

- *Mister Pip*
  Matilda is innocent, eager and intelligent; she experiences terrible things and nearly gives up on life, but gradually finds the strength to carry on.
- *To Kill a Mockingbird*
  Scout is clever, lively and strong-willed, but she has a hot temper. She matures during the novel, learning to hold back, show sympathy and live without prejudice.
- *Follow the Rabbit-Proof Fence*
  Gracie is shy, innocent and scared, but, from her wish to be reunited with her mother, she becomes braver and more independent.

Connectives of Comparison, Time or Consequence

When writing your answers, remember to use **connectives** to show the examiner that you understand a character is changing. These include:

- Connectives of **comparison**, e.g. Similarly, in contrast, in comparison.

- Connectives of **time**, e.g. At the beginning, after, later on, in Act 4.
- Connectives of **consequence**, e.g. Therefore, consequently, due to, as a result of.

Selecting and Analysing Quotations

When you make your points, you should provide **evidence** in the form of quotations. These quotations should support the point you are making and show what the character is like at the **start of the text** and how they **change by the end**.

You also need to make specific comments on how the language used in your quotations shows changing **characteristics**, as in the student responses on page 19.

Selecting and Analysing Quotations (Cont.)

Use a connective phrase to establish your first point

↓

Support your point with a quotation

↓

Analyse your quotation

Examine how the cultural context affects the character

Connective phrase establishing your next point and showing character development

Of Mice and Men

At the start of the novel, George seems hopeful of a better future, 'We'll have a big vegetable patch and a rabbit hutch and chickens. And when it rains in the winter, [...] we'll build up a fire in the stove'. The verb 'have', along with the list and repetition of 'and', shows that George is following the American Dream of owning his own land. It suggests he wants to be self-sufficient and the fire could symbolise a better future. The repetition of the pronoun 'we' shows he plans to share this life with Lennie.

We see these hopes destroyed at the end, before George kills Lennie, 'He said woodenly, 'If I was alone I could live so easy.' His voice was monotonous, had no emphasis.' The adjective and adverb linked to his voice, suggest he doesn't believe what he is saying. The contrasting repetition of the pronoun 'I', plus the word 'alone', suggests George knows his dreams of escaping the hardship of the Depression are over.

To Kill a Mockingbird

Early in the novel, we see how hot-tempered Scout is when she attacks Walter Cunningham: 'I was rubbing his nose in the dirt [...] I stomped at him to chase him away.' The active verbs 'rubbing' and, in particular, 'stomped' suggest her aggressive nature. Within the setting of the novel, this temper is viewed as especially bad because Scout is a girl and not conforming to traditional expectations of girls (an idea heightened by the fact she is beating up a boy).

By the end of the novel, Scout is maturing into a more reasoning and sympathetic person. After walking Boo Radley home, she says, 'Atticus was right. One time he said you never really know a man until you stand in his shoes and walk around in them.' This metaphor shows Scout developing empathy and links to her increased lack of prejudice in contrast with the community in which she lives.

Look at the two responses above and notice where the student has also made references to the text's **cultural context**. This is important, as you are showing the examiner that you understand how characterisation is affected by the text's context.

Try to find and analyse other quotations that show how the characters in the text that you've studied change. How do they change? Does the cultural context affect their decisions and how they change?

Quick Test

1. In the text you've studied, which character undergoes the biggest change? How?
2. Do the characters in the text that you've studied change for better or worse? Why?
3. What different things in the text that you've studied cause people to change?
4. Do any relationships in the text you've read change? In what ways?

1B Exploring Cultures: Themes

The Themes of the Text

You may be asked how an author presents a theme and develops it during their story. So, you need to know what the themes are in the text you're studying, for example:

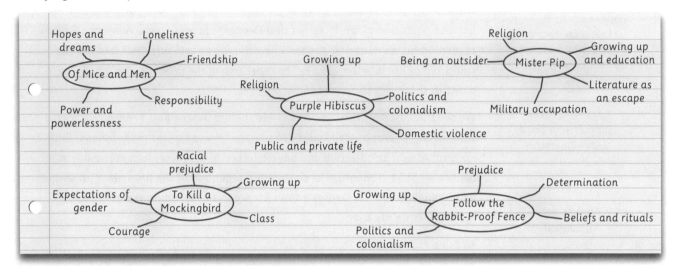

Where the Themes Appear

You need to be able to identify where the theme appears and how it's developed in the text you're studying. Themes can be explored through **characters** or **events**, but remember to consider how they link to the cultural context. For example:

- *Of Mice and Men*
  Power and powerlessness is explored through lots of the characters in the text. For example, Lennie has no social power but he has physical power. Meanwhile, Curley's wife has social power over Crooks (as a white person, and daughter of the boss), but is usually ignored because she is a woman.

- *Purple Hibiscus*
  Lots of different religions appear throughout the text: Papa's Catholicism, his father's ancestral Igbo beliefs, and Father Amadi's mix of Igbo tradition and modern Christianity. We see an extension of the latter, as Kambili begins to identify God with nature and family.

- *Mister Pip*
  The idea of being an outsider is explored through Mr Watts, the only white person remaining in Bougainville. Parallels are drawn between his life and that of Pip in *Great Expectations*.

- *To Kill a Mockingbird*
  Courage is explored through Atticus's commitment to justice, whatever the personal cost, and through Mrs Dubose's struggle with addiction. We also see courage in characters like Scout and Boo Radley, and the absence of courage in Bob Ewell.

- *Follow the Rabbit-Proof Fence*
  Prejudice can be seen in the early chapters, from the behaviour of white men towards the Aborigines. It is then explored through the attitudes of the Aborigines and the government towards mixed-race children.

How does the author present other themes in the text you're studying? Think about the different characters or events that illustrate these themes.

Analysing How Quotations Illustrate a Theme

It's important to support the points you're making about a theme with quotations. You need to select relevant quotations and **analyse** how that theme is presented through the author's choices of **language and structure**.

The following student response shows how to analyse quotations that link to the themes of a text:

Use a clear point to show how you are exploring the theme

Support it with a quotation as evidence

Make your point or idea clear

Evidence

Analyse how language or structure tells us something about the theme or cultural context

Analysis of quotation, linking to cultural context

Purple Hibiscus

Religion is explored through several characters. Papa has adopted post-colonial Catholicism and is disparaging of the ancestral beliefs of his own father, 'muttered about ignorant people participating in the ritual of pagan masquerades. He said that the stories about mmuo [...] were all devilish folklore'. The adjective 'ignorant', combined with the word 'masquerade', suggests traditional beliefs are foolish. Papa carries this further, though, when he adds the adjective 'devilish', suggesting, via his own Catholic beliefs, that these traditions are sinful and dangerous.

As Kambili grows up, she explores religion in a different way, 'I let my mind drift, imagining God laying out the hills of Nsukka with his wide white hands, crescent-moon shadows underneath his nails'. Here, in a link to the paganism that her father dislikes, God is being linked to nature. However, we can also see a symbol of the colonial influence of European Catholicism on her beliefs, in that she pictures God as a white man.

Quick Test

1. What do you think is the most important theme in the novel you've studied? Why do you think this?

2. Which events link to different themes? In what ways?

3. Which characters link to different themes? In what ways?

4. In the novel you've studied, are there any themes that cause conflict between characters? Why do they disagree?

Understanding the Question

Your question may read something like this:

> **(a)** Read the extract. How does the writer use description to present the characters of Lennie and Crooks?
>
> **(b)** How does the writer use the character of Crooks in the novel as a whole to present ideas about 1930s America?

You need to **read the question carefully** and note the **key words or phrases**. For example:

- Character and How: The examiner doesn't want you to just explain what the characters are like. You're expected to **pick out quotations** and say how you can tell what they're like from the words or punctuation being used.
- Novel as a whole: In part (b), you need to **refer to different parts of the book**.
- 1930s America: Here the examiner is asking you to think about the **novel's cultural context**.

Answering Part (a)

Annotate the extract by going through the text, **underlining** all the most important parts about the character or theme named in the task and **circling** the **most important words**, **punctuation and techniques** being used.

The examiner will expect you to do some **detailed analysis of language and structure**. Keep your quotations short and look out for different techniques to show off your understanding. Use a simple structure like PEA.

Answering Part (b)

Spend **two minutes planning** your response to part (b) noting down your ideas and the parts of the text you could refer to. Read through your ideas and number them in a **logical order**. Each of these can be a different paragraph of your response.

Don't waste too much time searching through the book for a specific line. Make sure you at least **refer to specific episodes** in the text. The most important thing is to **refer to aspects of the time and place** in which the story is set.

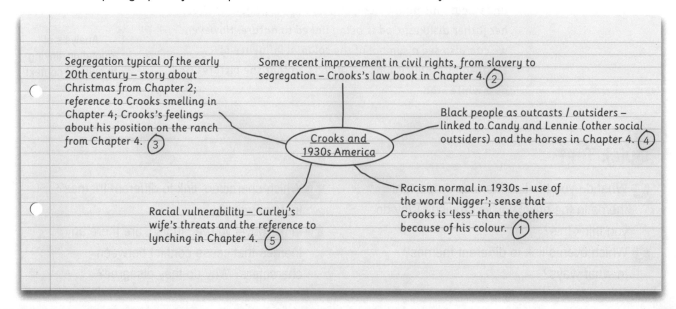

Segregation typical of the early 20th century – story about Christmas from Chapter 2; reference to Crooks smelling in Chapter 4; Crooks's feelings about his position on the ranch from Chapter 4. ③

Some recent improvement in civil rights, from slavery to segregation – Crooks's law book in Chapter 4. ②

Black people as outcasts / outsiders – linked to Candy and Lennie (other social outsiders) and the horses in Chapter 4. ④

Crooks and 1930s America

Racial vulnerability – Curley's wife's threats and the reference to lynching in Chapter 4. ⑤

Racism normal in 1930s – use of the word 'Nigger'; sense that Crooks is 'less' than the others because of his colour. ①

Unit 1 Section A

The accuracy of your spelling, punctuation and grammar is assessed in the following questions.

Sunlight on the Grass – Anthology

Foundation

Part (a)   How is Mrs Rutter presented in *The Darkness Out There*? Write about:
- what Mrs Rutter says and does
- the methods the writer uses.

Part (b)   Write about how one other character is presented in one other story from *Sunlight on the Grass*. Write about:
- what the character says and does
- the methods the writer uses.   *(34 marks)*

Higher

Part (a)   How does the writer present feelings in *My Polish Teacher's Tie*?

Part (b)   Write about how feelings are presented in one other story from *Sunlight on the Grass*.   *(34 marks)*

Lord of the Flies

Foundation

How do you respond to the character of Jack in the novel? Write about:
- what Jack says and does
- how others feel about him
- the methods the writer uses to present Jack.   *(34 marks)*

Higher

How does the writer present leadership in the novel?   *(34 marks)*

Martyn Pig

Foundation

How does the writer present the character of Alex? Write about:
- what Alex says and does
- how other characters treat her
- the methods the writer uses.   *(34 marks)*

Higher

How does the writer present Martyn's relationships with his dad and Jean?   *(34 marks)*

Touching the Void

Foundation

How do you respond to Simon in *Touching the Void*? Write about:
- what you feel about the things he says and does
- the methods the writer uses to present Simon.   *(34 marks)*

Higher

How does the writer make *Touching the Void* a tense and exciting book?   *(34 marks)*

The Woman in Black

Foundation

How does the writer make Eel Marsh House seem a frightening place? Write about:
- the surroundings of the house
- rooms in the house
- the methods the writer uses. *(34 marks)*

Higher

How do the first three chapters create atmosphere and suggest what is to come? *(34 marks)*

Under Milk Wood

Foundation

How does the writer present the village of Llareggub? Write about:

- what the village is like
- the methods the writer uses.
- how the villagers behave

(34 marks)

Higher

'I am a draper mad with love' says Mr Edwards. How does the writer present different types of love? *(34 marks)*

The Crucible

Foundation

How do you respond to the character of Reverend Hale? Write about:

- what you feel about the things he says and does
- the methods the writer uses to present Hale.

(34 marks)

Higher

How does the writer develop the relationship between John and Elizabeth? *(34 marks)*

Kindertransport

Foundation

Do you think *Kindertransport* is a sad play? Why? Write about:

- events that are upsetting
- the methods the writer uses to make the play moving.
- characters that you feel sorry for

(34 marks)

Higher

How is the theme of identity important in the play? *(34 marks)*

An Inspector Calls

Foundation

Who do you think is to blame for the death of Eva Smith? Write about:

- events that lead up to her suicide
- the methods the writer uses to suggest blame in the play.
- how different characters are responsible

(34 marks)

Higher

How does the writer create tension in the play? *(34 marks)*

Deoxyribonucleic Acid (DNA)

Foundation

How does the writer present peer pressure in the play? Write about:

- how peer pressure affects the behaviour or feelings of characters
- the methods the writer uses.

(34 marks)

Higher

How does the writer present the relationship between Lea and Phil? *(34 marks)*

Unit 1 Section B

The accuracy of your spelling, punctuation and grammar is assessed in the following questions.

Of Mice and Men

Read the following passage and then answer **Part (a)** and **Part (b)**.

Foundation

Part (a)   How does Steinbeck show the power that George has over Lennie in this passage?

Part (b)   How does Steinbeck show one other character using power in the novel? What does this tell you about the society in which the story is set? Write about:
- what the character says and does to show they have, or don't have, power
- the methods Steinbeck uses to show ideas about power.   *(34 marks)*

Higher

Part (a)   How does Steinbeck use details in this passage to explore the theme of power?

Part (b)   In the novel as a whole, how does Steinbeck present groups of people with and without power at the time?   *(34 marks)*

> Lennie hesitated, backed away, looked wildly at the brush line as though he contemplated running for his freedom. George said coldly, "You gonna give me that mouse or do I have to sock you?"
>
> "Give you what, George?"
>
> "You know God damn well what. I want that mouse."
>
> Lennie reluctantly reached into his pocket. His voice broke a little. "I don't know why I can't keep it. It ain't nobody's mouse. I didn't steal it. I found it lyin' right beside the road."
>
> George's hand remained outstretched imperiously. Slowly, like a terrier who doesn't want to bring a ball to its master, Lennie approached, drew back, approached again. George snapped his fingers sharply, and at the sound Lennie laid the mouse in his hand.
>
> "I wasn't doin' nothin' bad with it, George. Jus' strokin' in.
>
> George stood up and threw the mouse as far as he could into the darkening brush, and then he stepped to the pool and washed his hands. "You crazy fool. Don't you think I could see your feet was wet where you went across the river to get it?" He heard Lennie's whimpering cry and wheeled about. "Blubberin' like a baby! Jesus Christ! A big guy like you." Lennie's lip quivered and tears started in his eyes.

Mister Pip

Read the following passage and then answer **Part (a)** and **Part (b)**.

Foundation

Part (a)   How does Jones show us what Mr Watts is like and how he is treated?

Part (b)   How does Jones present different views about white people in the novel as a whole? Write about:
- what the characters say and do that show what they think of white people
- the methods Jones uses to get across different views about white people.   *(34 marks)*

Higher

Part (a)   In this passage, how does Jones present the character of Mr Watts?

Part (b)   How does Jones present different attitudes towards white people in the novel as a whole?

                    (34 marks)

Because Pop Eye was the only white for miles around, little kids stared at him until their ice blocks melted over their black hands. Older kids sucked in their breath and knocked on his door to ask to do their 'school project' on him. When the door opened some just froze and stared. I knew an older girl who was invited in; not everyone was. She said there were books everywhere. She asked him to talk about his life. She sat in a chair next to a glass of water he had poured for her, pencil in hand, notebook open. He said: 'My dear, there has been a great deal of it. I expect more of the same.' She wrote this down. She showed her teacher, who praised her initiative. She even brought it over to our house to show me and my mum, which is how I know about it.

It wasn't just for the fact he was the last white man that made Pop Eye what he was to us – a source of mystery mainly, but also confirmation of something else we held to be true.

We had grown up believing white to be the colour of all important things, like ice-cream, aspirin, ribbon, the moon, the stars. White stars and a full moon were more important when my grandfather grew up than they are now that we have generators.

Purple Hibiscus

Read the following passage and then answer **Part (a)** and **Part (b)**.

Foundation

Part (a) In this passage, how does Adichie show what Mama is like?

Part (b) In the novel as a whole, how does Adichie show what life was like for women at this time in Nigeria? Write about:

- what characters say and do that shows what women's lives were like
- different events that show what women's lives were like
- the methods Adichie uses to get this across.
                                                                                          (34 marks)

Higher

Part (a) How does Adichie present the character of Mama in this passage?

Part (b) In the novel as a whole, how does Adichie show what life was like for women in Nigeria at this time?
                                                                                          (34 marks)

Mama clucked in sympathy. "People do not always talk with sense. But it is good that the children go, especially the boys. They need to know their father's homestead and the members of their father's *umunna*."

"I honestly do not know how Ifediora came from an *umunna* like that."

I watched their lips move as they spoke; Mama's bare lips were pale compared to Aunty Ifeoma's, covered in a shiny bronze lipstick.

"*Umunna* will always say hurtful things," Mama said. "Did our own *umunna* not tell Eugene to take another wife because a man of his stature cannot have just two children? If people like you had not been on my side then …"

"Stop it, stop being grateful. If Eugene had done that, he would have been the loser, not you."

"So you say. A woman with children and no husband, what is that?"

"Me."

Mama shook her head. "You have come again, Ifeoma. You know what I mean. How can a woman live like that?" Mama's eyes had grown round, taking up more space on her face.

"*Nwunye m*, sometimes life begins when marriage ends."

"You and your university talk. Is this what you tell your students?" Mama was smiling.

"Seriously, yes. But they marry earlier and earlier these days. What is the use of a degree, they ask me, when we cannot find a job after graduation?"

"At least somebody will take care of them when they marry."

To Kill a Mockingbird

Read the following passage and then answer **Part (a)** and **Part (b)**.

Foundation

Part (a)   How does Lee use different descriptive details in this passage to show what the Ewell family are like?

Part (b)   How does Lee, in the novel as a whole, show us what Bob Ewell is like? Write about:

- what the character says and does
- what others characters say about him
- the methods Lee uses to show what he is like.   *(34 marks)*

Higher

Part (a)   In this passage, how does Lee present the Ewell family?

Part (b)   How does Lee, in the novel as whole, present the character of Bob Ewell?   *(34 marks)*

Every town the size of Maycomb had families like the Ewells. No economic fluctuations changed their status – people like the Ewells lived as guests of the county in prosperity as well as in the depths of a depression. No truant officers could keep their numerous offspring in school; no public health officer could free them from congenital defects, various worms, and the diseases indigenous to filthy surroundings.

Maycomb Ewells lived behind the town garbage dump in what was once a Negro cabin. The cabin's plank walls were supplemented with sheets of corrugated iron, its roof shingled with tin cans hammered flat, so only its general shape suggested its original design: square, with four tiny rooms opening on to a shotgun hall, the cabin rested uneasily upon four irregular lumps of limestone. Its windows were merely open spaces in the walls, which in the summertime were covered with greasy strips of cheesecloth to keep out the varmints that feasted on Maycomb's refuse.

The varmints had a lean time of it, for the Ewells gave the dump a thorough gleaning every day, and the fruits of their industry (those that were not eaten) made the plot of ground around the cabin look like the playhouse of an insane child: what passed for a fence was bits of tree-limbs, broomsticks and tool shafts, all tipped with rusty hammer-heads, snaggle-toothed rake heads, shovels, axes and grubbing hoes, held on with pieces of barbed wire. Enclosed by this barricade was a dirty yard containing the remains of a Model-T Ford (on blocks), a discarded dentist's chair, an ancient ice-box, plus lesser items: old shoes, worn-out table radios, picture-frames, and fruit jars, under which scrawny orange chickens pecked hopefully.

Follow the Rabbit-Proof Fence

Read the following passage and then answer **Part (a)** and **Part (b)**.

Foundation

Part (a) In this passage, how does Pilkington use details to show us different things about the Martu people (the traditional people of Australia) and their way of life?

Part (b) How does Pilkington bring out differences between groups of people in the novel as a whole? Write about:

- what groups of people are different to each other
- the methods Pilkington uses to show us these differences. *(34 marks)*

Higher

Part (a) How does Pilkington present the way of life of the Martu people (the traditional people of Australia) in this passage?

Part (b) How does Pilkington present differences between groups of people in the novel as a whole?

(34 marks)

They stood around in a circle, staring at the heap of clothing that the boss and the missus and others used to cover their bodies. The desert dwellers were baffled, they could not understand why anyone would be embarrassed or offended by their own nakedness: their normal, natural appearance. These people had roamed about in their own environment naked except for a pubic covering made from human hair. Their bodies were covered only with a salve, a mixture of red ochre and animal fat. This ointment is still believed to protect them from illness and evil spirits but its most common use is to disguise human body odour when hunting. Their bodies are also anointed during ceremonial occasions when their rituals are performed.

After supper, the group inspected the clothing before trying on anything. There was a lot of jesting and clowning going on when they paraded around before the amused onlookers. Gales of laughter rang out as old man Jibaru, the smallest man in the group, put on what must have been the largest trousers in the whole collection. Where and how was he expected to "make kumbu" as the waist came up under his armpits!

Each one had a set or two of clothes and nobody was interested whether they were stylish or fashionable so long as their bodies were covered. It didn't matter to anyone if the clothes were ill-fitting and uncomfortable, the important thing was that they were pleasing the boss and the missus.

Later that evening, someone suggested they might like to have a cool shower and change their clothes, but the group refused very strongly. They had just buried a family member and were still in mourning so they would wear the clothes over their ochre-covered bodies until the symbols painted on them disappeared.

Poetry Cluster from the Anthology: Introduction

What to Expect in the Exam

If you haven't written a controlled assessment essay comparing a series of poems, you'll be taking this exam. In **Unit 2, Section A** you'll have studied one of the four clusters from the anthology:

- Character and Voice
- Conflict
- Place
- Relationships

The question will name one poem from the cluster you've studied and you're expected to choose another poem from the same cluster to compare it to.

You'll be given a **choice of two questions** on the cluster of poems that you've studied. You'll need to answer one of these questions in **45 minutes**. You should read the question carefully, then spend **5 minutes planning** your ideas before you begin writing your response.

This **question** is worth 23% of your final GCSE mark.

How the Exam is Assessed

In this part of the exam, you're being examined on the following assessment objectives:

AO1	Respond to texts critically and imaginatively; select and evaluate relevant textual detail to illustrate and support interpretations.	40% of this question
AO2	Explain how language, structure and form contribute to writers' presentation of ideas, themes and settings.	20% of this question
AO3	Make comparisons and explain links between texts, evaluating writers' different ways of expressing meaning and achieving effects.	40% of this question

Comparison

It's very important that you actually compare the two poems. To make it clear to the examiner that you're comparing, you should use **connectives of comparison**. For example:

- In comparison
- Both
- Similarly
- Just as
- In contrast
- On the other hand
- However
- Whereas

Think about the **poems in groups or themes**. This will help you when you have to choose a poem and do comparisons. Remember, though, that a poem can be put into more than one group. Each time you group some of the poems together, think about how (not just what) key lines in each poem link to your theme.

When choosing two poems to compare, you should look at both their **similarities** and their **differences**.

Understanding the Poems

You'll need to be able to compare two poems and have a good understanding of:

- **Themes, ideas and issues**: how they are explored through the poem and portrayed to the reader.

- **Language, structure and form**: how the writer uses these techniques to convey meaning.

Language and Structure

In your analysis of poetry, you should always try to comment on the **effect of specific poetic techniques** that are being used by the writer. It's important that you get used to being able to spot these different techniques of **language and structure**. However, you shouldn't explore every technique that you spot, just the ones that relate to the question in the exam. Here are some ideas:

Technique	Description	Poem Example
Imagery – Simile	A simile is a description that **compares one thing to another**, using the words 'like' or 'as'. Writers use similes to help the reader **imagine** things.	In *The Farmer's Bride* (in the 'Relationships' section), similes are used to describe the unwilling bride: 'flying like a hare' and 'like a mouse'. The similes show her fear of the farmer, whether trying to escape or trying not to be noticed, as well as how she's been treated like an animal rather than a human. The repeated animal imagery could also suggest the farmer knows more about animals than he does about women.
Imagery – Metaphor	A metaphor is also a **comparison**, used to help the reader **imagine** things. However, it's written as if it's true (rather than using the words 'like' or 'as').	In *Les Grands Seigneurs* (from the 'Character and Voice' section), metaphors are used to show the speaker's past attitude towards men, 'Men were my buttresses, my castellated towers, / the bowers where I took my rest'. The metaphors suggest that she used men for protection and comfort, but on her own terms. She felt nothing for them; they were just objects to her.
Imagery – Personification	Personification is a type of metaphor, again used to help the reader imagine things. In personification, inanimate objects (such as a fridge) or abstract nouns (such as love) are **described as if they are human**.	Personification is used in *Futility* (from the 'Conflict' section) to describe the sunlight: 'If anything might rouse him now / The kind old sun will know'. The imagery shows how, in wartime, the heat of sunlight is valued ('kind'). But, by describing the sun as an old man, the poet suggests it's too weak, underlining the idea that nothing can help the dead soldier.
Imagery – Powerful Words	Sometimes an image provides a really good description or a contrast. Images can be created through the use of **powerful verbs** (doing words), **adjectives** (describing words) and **adverbs** (words that describe a verb).	Powerful language is used in *The Prelude* (in the 'Place' section) to convey the beauty of the lake, 'Small circles glittering idly in the moon, / […] sparkling light'. A verb, adverb and adjective are used to make the lake seem magical at night. The words show that the speaker sees the scene as peaceful and inspiring.
Alliteration	Alliteration is when poets begin several words that are close together with the same sound. This can make a **phrase stand out** or **emphasise a particular sound**. An aspect of alliteration is **sibilance**, where 's' sounds are used within a series of words.	In *Medusa* (from the 'Character and Voice' section), sounds are used to reflect the speaker's harshness, 'My bride's breath soured, stank / in the grey bags of my lungs' The alliterated 'b' is a hard, **plosive** sound that shows she has hardened. Her dangerous nature is emphasised by the sibilance, which also links to the Medusa's hissing snakes.

Technique	Description	Poem Example
Pattern of Three and Repetition	Repetition and pattern of three **emphasise ideas**, by saying them more than once or by grouping similar things together.	Repetition is used in *London* (from the 'Place' section) to emphasise social problems, 'In every cry of every man, / In every infant's cry of fear, / In every voice, in every ban'. The repetition of 'every' conveys the poet's belief that everyone suffers from oppression.
Short Sentences, Lists and Enjambment	Poets also use punctuation to **emphasise ideas**. A short sentence can make something stand out, whilst a list builds up ideas to make a point. **Enjambment** (carrying a sentence across a stanza) creates a dramatic pause that **emphasises particular words**.	The poem *Poppies* (from the 'Conflict' section) uses a list and enjambment to convey the speaker's feelings as her son leaves for war, 'All my words / flattened, rolled, turned into felt, // slowly melting.' The list builds up the idea that she cannot express her feelings. The enjambment changes the tone from frustration to sadness; it delays the end of the sentence to emphasise the last metaphor, reflecting the moment being lost and her words feeling useless.

Form

As well as thinking about the effects of language and structure on a poem, you should also try to consider the **poet's choice of form**.

Dramatic Monologue

A **dramatic monologue** is when the **poet takes on the voice of a character**. They appear to be addressing someone, but that person doesn't actually speak in the poem. This allows a poet to **explore someone else's perspective** in a more detailed way.

For example, *Horse Whisperer* (from 'Character and Voice'), *Out Of The Blue* (from 'Conflict') and *Sister Maude* (from 'Relationships').

Duologue is where two characters speak to each other, as in *The Ruined Maid* (from 'Character and Voice').

Sonnet

A **sonnet** is the **classic form of love poetry**. With 14 lines, 10 **syllables** per line, **iambic pentameter** rhythm, and a clear rhyme scheme, it is also quite a **tight, closed form** that **intensifies emotions**.

For example, *Ozymandias* (which features self-love, from 'Character and Voice'), *next to of course god america i* (from 'Conflict') and *Hour* (from 'Relationships').

Shape and Rhythm

Sometimes a poet isn't using a specific form, or is maybe using something that you don't recognise. If this is the case, you should still try to **comment on how the poem looks**.

For instance, is the poem in **stanzas** of a fairly even length (which suggests control) or are the stanzas all different lengths (which suggests greater freedom)?

Are there any stanzas that are unlike the others (for example, having fewer lines), as this might mean they're important?

Does the poem ignore usual punctuation and what is the effect of this (perhaps to speed the poem up, or to suggest freedom)?

2A Poetry Cluster: Character and Voice

Key Themes

In order to compare the poems in the 'Character and Voice' cluster of the Anthology, it's important to **explore the different themes** of the poems. Here are some of the key themes:

- Unusual characters
- Powerful emotions
- Voices and accents
- Solitary people

The following examples show how to form a response that compares two poems. Use the key below to explore the features of the example responses:

Point of comparison	Evidence
Analysis	Connective of comparison

Unusual Characters

Look at the unusual characters in the poems that you have studied and think about which poems you could compare using this theme.

Consider which lines of the poem show what is unusual about the character, and how this is shown through language or structure. You might compare *The Clown Punk* and *The River God*, for example:

> Both characters have a striking appearance. In 'The Clown Punk', he wears wild clothing, 'like a basket of washing that got up and walked'. This simile suggests that the clown looks odd and raggedy, but also somehow miraculous.
>
> In comparison, the river in 'The River God' is also messy, 'I may be smelly and I may be old, / Rough in my pebbles, reedy in my pools'. The four adjectives focus on the negative appearance of the river. However, the repetition of 'may' suggests that we should look beyond its appearance.

Powerful Emotions

There are lots of powerful emotions in the poems. Think about which lines show what the speaker is feeling, and how this is conveyed through language and structure. You could compare passionate love in *Singh Song!* with jealous love in *Medusa*, for example:

> Both speakers describe aspects of the person they love. In 'Singh Song!', he says his bride has, 'tiny eyes ov a gun / and di tummy of a teddy'. The two metaphors form a contrast that suggests, although she can be fierce, he finds her gentle and lovable.
>
> In contrast, the speaker in 'Medusa' presents the object of her love as, 'perfect man, Greek God, my own'. The pattern of three builds up the images to suggest she has an unrealistic vision of him. The final phrase 'my own' shows that this love is possessive.

Key Words   Simile • Adjective • Metaphor • Contrast • Pattern of three

Voices and Accents

Poets use different types of speech to convey characters. Consider how poems feature different voices and **accents**. Look at how the characters' styles of speech reveal different things about them.

You might want to compare how **non-standard English**, or **dialect** and accent, is used to present people to the reader *in Checking Out Me History* and *The Ruined Maid*, for example:

> In 'Checking Out Me History', the speaker uses dialect to show he values his Guyanese roots, 'Dem tell me about 1066 and all dat'. His non-standard English contrasts with the reference to English history, along with the dismissive phrase 'and all dat', to suggest there are more important things to him than English culture.
>
> In contrast, Amelia in 'The Ruined Maid' is happy to forget her roots, 'Your talking quite fits 'ee for high compa-ny!' –/ 'Some polish is gained with one's ruin,'. The two women's speech reflects Amelia's past and present. Her use of the formal pronoun 'one' and her haughty reference to 'polish', suggests she feels she has bettered herself.

Solitary People

Some of the poems feature people who seem lonely or isolated. Think about how the poet shows that the person is on their own, or doesn't fit in, and how this is conveyed through language and structure.

You could compare how the poets of *Brendon Gallacher* and *Give* make us feel about people who are on their own, for example:

> The speaker in 'Brendon Gallacher' makes us feel sorry for her when she describes the times with her imaginary friend, 'He would hold my hand and take me by the river / where we'd talk all about his family being poor.' The verbs 'hold' and 'take' suggests that she wanted to feel loved, whilst the reference to her talking about his family suggests she wanted to give love.
>
> In comparison, the speaker in 'Give' gains our sympathy as he has nothing, 'I'm on my knees. I beg of you.' The short sentences and simple language emphasise how basic and empty his life is, with both images showing his desperation and lack of social status.

Quick Test

1. Ask a friend to pick a poem from the cluster. Which other poem would you compare it to and why?
2. Which poems make effective use of similes or metaphors?
3. Which two poems do you think create the most memorable image of a character and why?
4. Which characters change during the poems, and how is this shown?

Key Themes

It's important to think about the different themes that occur throughout the poems in 'Place'. You may need to compare poems on the following key themes:

- Nature
- Weather
- Feelings about a place
- Places linked to an event or experience

The following examples show how to form a response that compares two poems. Use the key below to explore the features of the example responses:

Point of comparison   Evidence

Analysis   Connective of comparison

Nature

There are lots of poems in 'Place' in which you can compare nature as a theme. Think about how the poet uses the **language and structure** of the poem to explore the theme of nature. You might want to compare *The Prelude* and *Below the Green Corrie*, for example:

> Both poets present nature as alive and powerful. In 'The Prelude', Wordsworth describes a mountain, 'a huge peak, black and huge / As if with voluntary power instinct, / Upreared its head.' The use of personification makes the mountain seem alive, with the use of darkness and the repetition of the adjective 'huge' adding a sense of strength and danger.
>
> Similarly, MacCaig uses personification to describe the mountains as alive in 'Below The Green Corrie': 'The mountains gathered round me / like bandits. Their leader / swaggered up close in the dark light, / full of threats, full of thunders.' The use of simile ('like bandits'), metaphor ('full of thunders') and verbs ('gathered', 'swaggered') help to create an image of power and threat; like Wordsworth, this is added to by the use of darkness.

Weather

The poems in 'Place' often feature the weather. Explore which poems feature weather as a theme and the poetic techniques used to describe the weather. You could compare *Spellbound* and *Storm in the Black Forest*, for example:

> Both poets describe the weather as fierce and frightening. In 'Spellbound', she describes how, 'The wild winds coldly blow'. The use of alliteration emphasises the power of the storm, whilst the adverb helps the reader to imagine how horrible the storm feels.
>
> In comparison, 'Storm in the Black Forest' focuses on lightning, 'a still brighter white snake wriggles among it, spilled / and tumbling wriggling down the sky: / and then the heavens cackle with uncouth sounds.' The snake metaphor reflects the danger of the lightning, whilst the verbs and repetition show its untamed power. This is emphasised by the use of personification at the end to describe the thunder, with the reference to 'the heavens' also adding to the sense of nature's awesome power.

Personification • Simile • Metaphor • Alliteration

Feelings about a Place

In some of the poems, the poets describe how they feel about a place. Here you might compare how they feel about a **country, region, town or building** that they visit, or in which they live. Think about which poems show how someone feels about a place and whether it is portrayed in a positive or negative light. Consider how the poets' feelings are shown through their choices of language and structure. You could compare *Hard Water* and *London*, for example:

> In 'Hard Water', the poet links her feelings for the North to the taste of the water, 'I loved coming home to this. / Flat. Straight. Like the vowels, / like the straight talk: hey up me duck'. The verb 'loved' shows her feelings straight away. She explains her feelings through the similes and short sentences, suggesting the honesty and bluntness of her town and its people. This is emphasised by the colloquial dialect to suggest friendliness.
>
> In contrast, Blake seems horrified by the state of his city, 'How the chimney-sweeper's cry / Every black'ning church appals'. This is a reference to child labour of the industrial age. The poet uses a metaphor to blame the church for not helping and, through simple symbolism of darkness, suggests that the city has lost its goodness.

Places Linked To an Event or Experience

Several of the poems in the 'Place' cluster describe an **event or experience** and how it is linked to a certain place. You could compare *Cold Knap Lake* and *Neighbours* by Gillian Clarke, for example:

> In 'Cold Knap Lake', the near-tragedy is described through the effects of the water, 'Blue-lipped and dressed in water's long green silk / she lay for dead'. The first use of colour describes the effect of the cold water, whilst the metaphor for the wet clothes and weeds suggests the horror of the girl's awful stillness.
>
> Nature is again linked to tragedy in 'Neighbours', exploring the effects of the Chernobyl disaster on the world: 'This spring a lamb sips caesium on a Welsh hill'. The peaceful images of nature are contrasted with the more dangerous side of the natural world ('caesium'), and the effects of humankind. Sibilance is used to create a threatening tone as the lamb innocently poisons itself.

Quick Test

1. Ask a friend to pick a poem from the cluster. Which other poem would you compare it to and why?
2. Which poems make effective use of similes or metaphors?
3. Which two poems do you think create the most memorable image of a place and why?
4. Which poems describe places in a positive way, and which in a negative way?

Key Themes

Many poems have been written about conflicts around the world. You should consider the following key themes:

- Different feelings about conflict
- Different experiences of conflict
- How conflict affects people's lives
- Patriotism

The following examples show how to form a response that compares two poems. Use the key below to explore the features of the example responses:

Point of comparison   Evidence

Analysis   Connective of comparison

Different Feelings about Conflict

Poems often describe **how people feel about different conflicts**. Explore which poems display feelings about conflict and how the poet **conveys** these

feelings. You might compare *Mametz Wood* and *Hawk Roosting,* for example:

> The two poets present different views of conflict. In 'Mametz Wood', Owen Shears conveys sadness at the death of soldiers during the First Battle of the Somme, 'the china plate of a shoulder blade, / the relic of a finger, the blown / and broken bird's egg of a skull'. The metaphors create sadness by conveying how delicate and precious these soldiers were. The list of different body parts builds up a sense of horror at their slaughter, with the plosives throughout the sentence reflecting the gunfire the men faced.
>
> In contrast, 'Hawk Roosting' imagines a bird of prey's pleasure in killing, 'My manners are tearing off heads – / The allotment of death'. Like Shears, Hughes uses metaphor to convey slaughter. The ironic reference to 'manners', juxtaposed with the aggressive verb 'tearing', emphasises how much the hawk enjoys killing.

Different Experiences of Conflict

The poems address conflicts from various times and places. You might want to look at how the poets convey **different experiences of conflict**.

For this theme, you could compare *Belfast Confetti* and *The Charge of the Light Brigade,* for example:

> Both poets describe the horror of conflict. In 'Belfast Confetti', the poet describes his experience of metal being thrown during a riot, 'Suddenly as the riot squad moved in it was raining exclamation marks, / Nuts, bolts, nails, car keys'. The use of the adverb and the metaphor suggest the shock and noise for a civilian caught up in conflict. The list form builds up a sense of chaos and the feeling that it isn't going to stop.
>
> In comparison, Tennyson imagines the experiences of soldiers in 'The Charge of the Light Brigade': 'Cannon to the right of them, / Cannon to the left of them, / Cannon in front of them / Volley'd and thunder'd'. Again, the poet focuses on noise and shock, using powerful verbs to help the reader imagine the scene. Anaphora and list form are used to build up the idea that these men feel surrounded and are fighting against the odds.

Metaphor • Plosive • Ironic • Juxtaposition • Anaphora

How Conflict Affects People's Lives

Some poets turn their attention to how people are affected by conflict. Think about which poems show how conflict affects people's lives and how this is shown through the use of different poetic techniques. You could compare *Poppies* and *At the Border, 1979,* for example:

> In 'Poppies', the speaker reflects on the loss of her son during the war, 'All my words / flattened, rolled, turned into felt, // slowly melting. I was brave'. The list of metaphors builds up a sense that she couldn't quite say what she wanted to her son before he left to fight. The enjambment creates a pause to emphasise her inability to say what she means. The comment about bravery adds the idea that it isn't just the soldiers who have to show courage, it is also their loved ones.
>
> 'At the Border, 1979', explores the effects of conflict in a different way, showing people returning home after exile, 'She said that the roads are much cleaner / the landscape is more beautiful / and people much kinder'. The pattern of three and the intensifiers suggest the mother's happiness at returning home, whilst also alluding (especially 'much kinder') to the life they have led whilst in exile.

Patriotism

Several of these poems examine the strong feelings that people have for their country. Look at poems that explore patriotism and think about how it is conveyed by the ways the poets write. You could compare *Flag* and *next to of course god america i,* for example:

> The two poets explore different responses to patriotism. In 'Flag', the poet writes, 'What's that unfurling from a pole? / It's just a piece of cloth / that makes the guts of men grow bold.' The question and the adverb ('just') suggest that flags mean nothing to some people, whilst the metaphor describes how for others they stir strong feelings of patriotism.
>
> In comparison, 'next to of course god america i' explores how strong patriotism can be mindless, 'thy sons acclaim your glorious name by gorry / by jingo by gee by gosh by gum / why talk of beauty'. By running together and rhyming different soundbites, omitting punctuation, mixing religious language ('thy') and silly colloquialisms ('by jingo'), the poet warns against the speaker's blind patriotism by making it sound nonsense.

Quick Test

1. Choose a poem from 'Conflict'. Which other poem would you compare it to and why?
2. Which poems make effective use of similes or metaphors?
3. Which two poems do you think create the most memorable image of conflict and why?
4. Which two poems do you think convey emotions in the most powerful way and why?

Key Themes

The poems in the 'Relationships' poetry cluster are often centred on the following key themes:

- Romantic love
- Sex and passion
- Family ties
- Problems in relationships

The following examples show how to form a response that compares two poems. Use the key below to explore the features of the example responses:

Point of comparison	Evidence
Analysis	Connective of comparison

Romantic Love

In the 'Relationships' poetry cluster, you should look at how different poets present romantic love in their poems.

Consider what is being said about love, and how this is achieved through language or structure. For example, you could compare *Hour* and *Sonnet 43*:

> The two sonnets both convey how much the speaker loves someone. In 'Hour' the poet says that, 'love spins gold, gold, gold from straw'. The metaphor and repetition suggest that loving someone makes everything amazing; even the smallest moments together ('straw') are valuable and precious ('gold'). The allusion to Rumplestiltskin also suggests that their love is like a fairy tale.
>
> In comparison, in 'Sonnet 43', Browning writes: 'I love thee to the depth and breadth and height / My soul can reach'. Again, repetition is being used to emphasise how strong her love is. This is added to by the reference to her 'soul', which suggests her love is endless and immeasurable.

Sex and Passion

Several of the poems about love aren't really romantic; they focus more on **desire**. Consider which poems focus on sex and passion.

Think about how this is explored through the ways the poets write. For this theme, you could compare *In Paris with You* and *To His Coy Mistress*, for example:

> Both poets focus on sex and passion, rather than romantic love. In 'In Paris With You', the speaker wants to stay in bed with the girl he has met, 'If we say sod off to sodding Notre Dame, / If we skip the Champs Elysees / And remain here in this sleazy / Old hotel room'. The colloquialisms and repetition of coarse language seem immediately unromantic. This is added to by his dismissal of romantic tourist spots, in favour of (suggested by the adjective 'sleazy') casual sex.
>
> 'To His Coy Mistress' is similarly unromantic in its attempt to talk a girl into bed, 'then worms shall try / That long preserved virginity, / And your quaint honour turn to dust'. Imagining the girl's death isn't very romantic, whilst the adjectives ('long preserved' and 'quaint') show the speaker's frustration that she will not sleep with him.

Family Ties

Some of the poems in the cluster focus on **family relationships**, such as their feelings for a parent or a sibling.

Consider how the different feelings about family members are shown through the poets' choices of language and structure. You could compare *Praise Song for My Mother* and *Harmonium*, for example:

> In 'Harmonium', the speaker compares his father with a church organ, 'yellowed the fingernails of its keys. / And one of its notes had lost its tongue, / And holes were worn in both the treadles'. The images (built up by the repetition of 'and') reflect how his father is getting old, but that he still wants and cares for him. The double meaning of 'lost its tongue' also suggests that his father isn't very communicative.
>
> 'Praise Song for My Mother' also uses repetition of 'and' to build up an image of the speaker's parent, 'You were / water to me / deep and bold and fathoming'. The metaphor and pattern of three suggest that her mother is powerful and mysterious. The use of water could be to suggest that the speaker could not have survived without her.

Problems in Relationships

Some of the poems explore how some relationships can be negative or problematic. Consider which poems explore problems in a relationship and how the poets conveys this. You could compare *Sister Maude* and *Brothers*, for example:

> The two poems explore the idea of not getting along with a sibling. In 'Sister Maude', the speaker has been betrayed by her sister: 'Who told my father of my dear? / Oh who but Maude, my sister Maude, / Who lurked to spy and peer'. The three verbs present Maude as nasty and untrustworthy. The way in which the poet answers her opening question with an exclamation ('Oh') and repetition of her sister's name suggests shock, but perhaps also realisation that she should have expected it.
>
> In contrast, the little boy in 'Brothers' is nice but the speaker finds him irritating, 'Saddled with you for the afternoon… / while you skipped beside us in your ridiculous tank top'. The colloquial verb 'saddled' suggests he found his little brother a burden. The verb and adjective used to describe the boy also suggest he found him embarrassing in his childish behaviour and unfashionable clothes.

Quick Test

1. Pick a poem from the cluster. Which other poem would you compare it to and why?
2. Which poems make effective use of similes or metaphors?
3. Which two poems do you think explore a relationship in the most interesting way and why?
4. Which two poems do you think convey emotions in the most powerful way and why?

2A Poetry Cluster: Approaching the Question

Understanding the Question

In the exam for **Unit 2, Section A**, you'll be asked to **compare two poems from the poetry cluster** that you have studied. Your question may read something like this:

> Compare the ways poets present the weather in *Wind* and one other poem from the 'Place' section.

You need to **read the question carefully** and note the **key words or phrases**. For example:

- Compare: It's important that, throughout your answer, you **make comparisons about the two texts**. Don't just write about one poem, followed by the other.

- The ways and present: Don't just describe the poem. You're expected to **pick out quotations** and say how **specific words**, **punctuation** or **techniques** are being used to show things to the reader.

- Weather: In the exam, you'll be given a specific focus. You aren't writing everything you know about two poems, you're **exploring one aspect of two poems** (in this case, the presentation of weather).

- One other: Although the question will tell you one of the poems you must use, **you'll have to choose another poem that links to the theme** by yourself.

Making Your Plan

Spend five minutes planning your ideas. Remember, you can **make notes around the poems** in the anthology once the exam begins. **Keep focused** on what the question is asking you.

Work out which points go together so you're **comparing** in your essay; this can be **similarities or differences**. Try to **number your points in a logical order** so you write an essay that flows in a **clear and sensible way**.

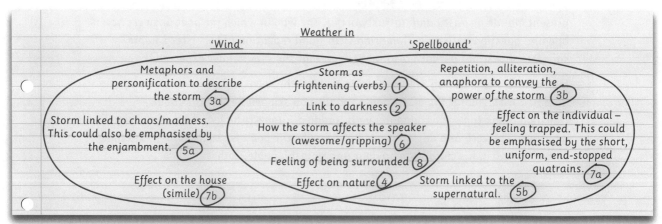

Answering the Question

Follow your plan and try to **use a clear structure**, for example, PEA. Pick 'good' quotations from the poems that allow you to **comment on words, punctuation and techniques**.

To make it clear that you're comparing the poems, remember to **link your ideas together using different connectives**. For example: similarly, in comparison, just as, however, in contrast, this is different in.

What to Expect in the Exam

In **Unit 2, Section B** you'll be given **one question**, based on an 'unseen' poem (one that isn't in the *Moon on the Tides* anthology), and you'll have **30 minutes** to complete your response.

The question will ask you to **analyse how a theme or idea is conveyed in the poem**, through the **writer's choices of language, structure and form**.

If you're doing the **foundation paper**, the question will be split into **two parts** to help you:
- **Part (a)** will ask you about the theme or idea.
- **Part (b)** will ask you how this is being conveyed.

If you're taking the **higher paper**, the question will not be split into two parts.

You should read the question carefully, then spend **5 minutes annotating** the poem and **ordering your ideas** before you begin writing your response.

This **question** is worth 12% of your final GCSE mark.

How the Exam is Assessed

In this part of the exam, you're being examined on the following assessment objectives:

AO1	Respond to texts critically and imaginatively; select and evaluate relevant textual detail to illustrate and support interpretations.	50% of this question
AO2	Explain how language, structure and form contribute to writers' presentation of ideas, themes and settings.	50% of this question

Understanding Your Text

Whichever poem you are given in the exam, you'll need to use the same skills that you have developed while studying for Section A:
- **Themes, ideas and issues**: how they are explored through the poem and portrayed to the reader.
- **Language, structure and form**: how the writer uses these techniques to achieve different effects.

Analysing a Poem

The best way to explore a new poem is to think about the following things:

- **Themes**: what is the poem about? What ideas and issues does the poet address?
- **Imagery**: how does the poet describe things? What poetic techniques are used to convey meaning?
- **Form**: do you notice anything about the type of poem, or its shape and rhythm?

- **Structure**: How are the **stanzas** structured? Is the length of the sentences, or the use of punctuation, important?

If it helps, try to remember: **TIFS**

You may also be asked to give your **own opinions** on the poem and **how effective** it is. This is best done at the end of your answer, in a mini conclusion.

Analysing Poetry Using TIFS

Here is an example of a modern poem, *Hitcher* by Simon Armitage:

- **Read through the poem carefully**.
- Think about **themes, imagery, form and structure**.

- Use the commentary on these pages to help you **analyse the poem** or to check your progress.
- Use the quick test questions to help shape your **personal response** to the poem.

Hitcher by Simon Armitage

I'd been tired, under
the weather, but the ansaphone kept screaming:
One more sick-note, mister, and you're finished. Fired.
I thumbed a lift to where the car was parked.
A Vauxhall Astra. It was hired.

I picked him up in Leeds.
He was following the sun to west from east
with just a toothbrush and the good earth for a bed. The truth,
he said, was blowin' in the wind,
or round the next bend.

I let him have it
on the top road out of Harrogate – once
with the head, then six times with the krooklok
in the face – and didn't even swerve.
I dropped it into third

and leant across
to let him out, and saw him in the mirror
bouncing off the kerb, then disappearing down the verge.
We were the same age, give or take a week.
He said he liked the breeze

to run its fingers
through his hair. It was twelve noon.
The outlook for the day was moderate to fair.
Stitch that, I remember thinking,
you can walk from there.

Themes

Poets explore various **ideas and issues**. You need to be able to work out what the poem is about:

- Stanzas 1 and 2 tell us that the speaker is a fairly average man who picks up a hitchhiker.
- In the next two stanzas, he kills the hitchhiker for apparently no reason.
- In the last stanza he makes a joke about what he has done.
- The themes or ideas in the poem are violence, dissatisfaction, and freedom versus feeling trapped.

Imagery

You need to consider how the poet uses **images or description**. This will probably take up the majority of your answer.

- Stanza 1 uses **colloquial** language ('under the weather'), familiar images ('Vauxhall Astra') and familiar feelings (not wanting to go to work) to make the speaker seem an ordinary, unremarkable person. So, when he kills the hitchhiker we are shocked. The normality could also suggest that this murder isn't a one-off.
- Stanza 2 uses images of freedom ('following the sun', 'the good earth for a bed'), to suggest that the hitcher is relaxed and carefree. The **personification** in the last two stanzas adds to this impression. This forms a contrast with the speaker's life, as described in stanza 1, which may give us a motive for the murder: jealousy.
- Stanzas 3 and 4 use violent imagery to shock the reader and show us what the speaker's really like ('once / with the head, then six times with the krooklok'). He seems callous in how he sees the man as worthless, 'bouncing off the kerb'.
- In the last stanza, the speaker uses a double meaning ('stitch that', meaning 'I'm not having that' but also a reference to hitting someone) and a sarcastic comment to create humour, as if he thinks what he has done is funny.

Form

Try to consider how the **form of the poem** helps to convey its meaning.

- The form of the poem is a **dramatic monologue**: the poet takes on the role of a character. This allows the reader to get inside the speaker's head.
- The poem is made up of five stanzas, each with five lines. Although the lines differ in length, the stanzas look similar: the lines get longer until line 3, and then they get shorter. These things combine to reflect how the speaker feels trapped in his life and his sense of routine.
- The first two stanzas are end-stopped (they end with a full stop), but the third and fourth stanzas run on, using **enjambment**. This could be done to suggest that he only feels free when he kills.

Structure

Comment on how the **structure or punctuation of the poem** helps to convey its meaning.

- The poet uses lots of short sentences, which makes them sound very blunt. This reflects the speaker's boredom with his own life. It also contrasts with the longer, more descriptive sentence about the killing, which suggests he feels more alive when he kills.
- The use of a **parenthesis** in the form of two dashes in the third stanza creates a pause before ' – and didn't even swerve' which helps to make the poem disturbing by emphasising how he seems pleased with himself.

Quick Test

1. What do you think of the speaker?
2. What reasons does the speaker seem to have for the murder?
3. How do you respond to the end of the poem?
4. Why might Armitage have written this poem?

Analysing a Poem

The 'unseen' poem that you're asked to analyse could be from the **English Literary Heritage**.

Analysing these poems can be more difficult than modern poetry because the **language seems old** **and can be used differently**. However, you should still focus on exploring the **TIFS**:

- **Themes**
- **Imagery**
- **Form**
- **Structure**

Analysing Poetry Using TIFS

Here is an example of a poem from the Literary Heritage, *Remember* by Christina Rossetti:

- **Read the poem carefully**.
- As you read it, think about **themes, imagery, form and structure**.
- Use the commentary on these pages to help you **analyse the poem** or to check your progress.
- Use the quick test questions to help shape your **personal response** to the poem.

Remember **by Christina Rossetti**

Remember me when I am gone away,
Gone far away into the silent land;
When you can no more hold me by the hand,
Nor I half turn to get yet turning stay.
Remember me when no more day by day
You tell me of our future that you planned:
Only remember me; you understand
It will be late to counsel then or pray.
Yet if you should forget me for a while
And afterwards remember, do not grieve:
For if the darkness and corruption leave
A vestige* of the thoughts that once I had,
Better by far you should forget and smile
Than you should remember and be sad.

* vestige = a trace or small reminder of something.

Themes

- Lines 2 and 3 tell us that the speaker's talking to her lover and imagining what will happen after she has died.
- The first half of the poem mentions how small things are important in a relationship.
- The second half focuses on the idea of grief and how she doesn't want her lover to be unhappy when she has gone.
- She wants to be remembered, but in a good – not painful – way.

Imagery

- The first two lines use **euphemisms** for death ('gone away', 'silent land'), which shows the speaker wants to make her death seem less final and painful.
- There is a romantic image in line 3 ('hold me by the hand').
- Small images of their life together are included ('day by day', 'I half turn to go') to suggest that each moment they spent together was precious.
- The poet includes an image of hopes being lost ('our future that you planned') to build up the feeling of grief.
- Commands ('do not grieve') are used to show she doesn't want him to be unhappy.

- The imagery becomes more negative towards the end ('darkness and corruption'), to acknowledge that death is final.
- The final **couplet juxtaposes** opposite images to suggest what he could do after her death ('remember and be sad') and what he should do ('forget and smile'), which shows how much she cares for him.

Form

- The form of the poem is a **sonnet**, which is a traditional form for love poetry.
- The tight, closed form of a sonnet (only 14 lines, 10 syllables per line, and a clear rhyme scheme), makes the emotion more intense. It also reflects the idea that death is inescapable.

Structure

- The poet uses quite a lot of repetition. The **pronoun** 'you' is repeated, which suggests the person being addressed is important to the speaker, as is *Remember* to show that their relationship is strong.
- The words 'away' and 'no more' are also repeated to emphasise the idea of life coming to an end.

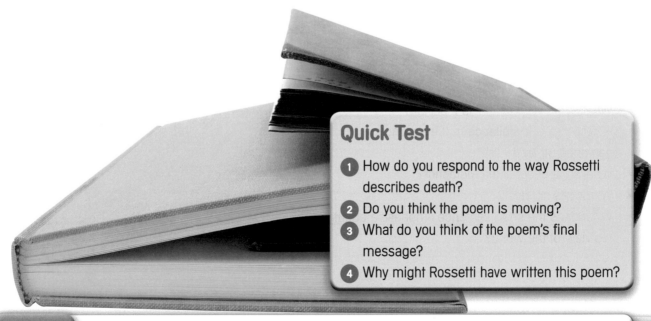

Quick Test

1. How do you respond to the way Rossetti describes death?
2. Do you think the poem is moving?
3. What do you think of the poem's final message?
4. Why might Rossetti have written this poem?

Annotation

When you're given an unseen poem to analyse in the exam, it's a good idea to quickly **annotate the poem** rather than try to write about it straight away. This means making **notes around the poem** about the different things you spot.

You need to **keep focused on the theme** that the exam question has asked you to explore, and you should try to cover the different parts of TIFS.

Using TIFS in Your Annotations

Look at the poem *Stealing* by Carol Ann Duffy on the next page. If this were to appear as an unseen poem in the exam, the examiner might ask you:

- How does the poet present the speaker in *Stealing*?

or

- What do you think the poet is saying about crime in this poem? How is this achieved through the way that she writes?

or

- Do you think this is a sympathetic portrayal of a criminal? Explain your views, referring to the writer's choices of language, structure and form.

The first stanza of the poem has been annotated for you, to show the sort of things that you might be picking out if you were reading it in the exam.

Below, are some questions relating to the remaining four stanzas. This is so you can have a go at annotating the poem on your own. Afterwards, you could try answering one of the sample exam questions from above.

Stanza 2
- What is his view of life? Is it selfish?
- What might the **sibilance** in the second sentence be for?
- What's the effect of the metaphor?
- Why does he steal?
- What does the short sentence emphasise about his view of the world?

Stanza 3
- Why does he steal? What does he get from it?
- Could 'nowhere' have a double meaning?
- How does the metaphor describe his life as a thief?
- How do the mirrors suggest why he steals?
- How does the breath on the mirror **symbolise** his limited effect on society as a thief?

Stanza 4
- Why does he destroy the snowman? How old does this make him seem – why?
- What do the short sentences, repetition, powerful **colloquial verb**, and metaphor suggest about him? How do they make him seem?
- How does the last sentence make him seem? How do you respond to this?

Stanza 5
- What is the effect of the short sentence?
- How is this emphasised by the metaphor?
- What could the other two objects that he has stolen symbolise?
- What does the **rhetorical question** suggest about his feelings? Who might this question be directed at?

Using TIFS in Your Annotations (Cont.)

Question and answer = dramatic monologue. The poet grabs our attention by making us feel part of a conversation.

Simile and metaphor show he relates to the snowman's coldness; he's unfeeling/lonely.

Stealing **by Carol Ann Duffy**

The most unusual thing I ever stole? A snowman.
Midnight. He looked magnificent; a tall, white mute
beneath the winter moon. I wanted him, a mate
with a mind as cold as the slice of ice
within my own brain. I started with the head.

Better off dead than giving in, not taking
what you want. He weighed a ton; his torso,
frozen stiff, hugged to my chest, a fierce chill
piercing my gut. Part of the thrill was knowing
that children would cry in the morning. Life's tough.

Sometimes I steal things I don't need. I joy-ride cars
to nowhere, break into houses just to have a look.
I'm a mucky ghost, leave a mess, maybe pinch a camera.
I watch my gloved hand twisting the doorknob.
A stranger's bedroom. Mirrors. I sigh like this – *Aah.*

It took some time. Reassembled in the yard,
he didn't look the same. I took a run
and booted him. Again. Again. My breath ripped out
in rags. It seems daft now. Then I was standing
alone amongst lumps of snow, sick of the world.

Boredom. Mostly I'm so bored I could eat myself.
One time, I stole a guitar and thought I might
learn to play. I nicked a bust of Shakespeare once,
flogged it, but the snowman was strangest.
You don't understand a word I'm saying, do you?

Short sentences to set the scene.

Alliteration of 'm' – reflects pleasure in stealing the snowman (mmm).

Adjectives show he's impressed by the snowman.

Key Words   Dramatic monologue • Alliteration • Adjective • Simile • Metaphor   47

2A/B Exam Practice Questions

Unit 2 Section A

Character and Voice

Foundation

Poets sometimes use a speaker to narrate a poem. Compare how poets present the speaker in *Medusa* and in **one** other poem from 'Character and Voice'. Remember to compare:

* what the speakers are like
* how the poets present the speakers by the ways they write. *(36 marks)*

Higher

Compare the ways poets present women in *The Ruined Maid* and in **one** other poem from 'Character and Voice'. *(36 marks)*

Place

Foundation

Compare how poets present their feelings about a place in *London* and in **one** other poem from 'Place'. Remember to compare:

* what the poets think and feel about the place
* how the poets present these thoughts and feelings by the ways they write. *(36 marks)*

Higher

Compare how poets use language to present ideas in *Hard Water* and in **one** other poem from 'Place'. *(36 marks)*

Conflict

Foundation

Compare how poets present the idea of being under attack in *Belfast Confetti* and in **one** other poem from 'Conflict'. Remember to compare:

* what it's like to be in the middle of conflict
* how the poets present what it's like by the ways they write. *(36 marks)*

Higher

Compare how poets present ideas about conflict in *The Right Word* and in **one** other poem from 'Conflict'. *(36 marks)*

Relationships

Foundation

Compare how poets present romantic love in *Sonnet 43* and in **one** other poem from 'Relationships'. Remember to compare:

* what romantic thoughts and feelings are conveyed
* how the poets presents these thoughts and feelings by the ways they write. *(36 marks)*

Higher

Compare how poets present family relationships in *Brothers* and in **one** other poem from 'Relationships'. *(36 marks)*

Read the poem below and answer the questions that follow:

Blessing by Imtiaz Dharker

The skin cracks like a pod.
There never is enough water.

Imagine the drip of it,
the small splash, echo
in a tin mug,
the voice of a kindly god.

Sometimes, the sudden rush
of fortune. The municipal pipe bursts,
silver crashes to the ground
and the flow has found
a roar of tongues. From the huts,
a congregation: every man woman
child for streets around
butts in, with pots,
brass, copper, aluminium,
plastic buckets,
frantic hands,

and naked children
screaming in the liquid sun,
their highlights polished to perfection,
flashing light,
as the blessing sings
over their small bones.

Foundation

Part (a)   This poem is set in an Indian town where there is a shortage of water. What ideas about water does the poet explore?

Part (b)   How are these ideas shown by the way the poet writes about the water?   *(18 marks)*

Higher

What techniques does the poet use to show how precious water is in the Indian town?   *(18 marks)*

Read the poem below and answer the questions that follow:

Sonnet by John Clare, 1841.

I love to see the summer beaming forth
And white wool sack clouds sailing to the north
I love to see the wild flowers come again
And Mare blobs stain with gold the meadow drain
And water lilies whiten on the floods
Where reed clumps rustle like a wind shook wood
Where from her hiding place the Moor Hen pushes
And seeks her flag nest floating in bull rushes
I like the willow leaning half way o'er
The clear deep lake to stand upon its shore
I love the hay grass when the flower head swings
To summer winds and insects happy wings
That sport about the meadow the bright day
And see bright beetles in the clear lake play

* Mare blobs = small yellow flowers

Foundation

Part (a) What different things does the poet like about the summer?

Part (b) How does he use language, structure and form to show what he likes about summer?   *(18 marks)*

Higher

What are the poet's feelings about summer and what techniques does he use to convey them?   *(18 marks)*

What to Expect in the Exam

If you haven't written a controlled assessment essay on a Shakespeare play, you'll be taking this exam. In **Unit 4, Section A** you'll be given a **choice of two questions** on the play that you've studied. You'll need to **answer one** of these questions in **50 minutes**.

Your question will be in **two parts**:

- **Part (a)** will ask you to analyse how a character or theme is presented in an extract from the play that you've studied. Read the question carefully, then spend **3–5 minutes annotating the extract** and **drawing your ideas together** before you begin writing your response. Spend **20–25 minutes** writing your answer before moving onto part (b).

- **Part (b)** will ask you to explore how the same character or theme is presented at one other point in the play. Read the question carefully, then spend **3–5 minutes choosing the scene** you are going to use and **planning your ideas** before you start writing.

This **question** is worth 20% of your final GCSE mark.

How the Exam is Assessed

In this part of the exam, you're being examined on the following assessment objectives:

AO1	Respond to texts critically and imaginatively; select and evaluate relevant textual detail to illustrate and support interpretations.	50% of this question
AO2	Explain how language, structure and form contribute to writers' presentation of ideas, themes and settings.	50% of this question

Understanding Your Text

Whichever Shakespeare play you're studying, you'll need to have a good understanding of:

- **Characters**: who the main characters are, how they act and why.
- **Setting**: where and when the play is set, and its effect on the characters and their lives.
- **Context**: how the play relates to its social, historical and cultural context.
- **Themes**: how ideas and issues are explored in the play and portrayed to the reader.
- **Language, structure and form**: how Shakespeare uses these techniques to achieve different effects.
- **Stagecraft**: how the play is performed on stage.

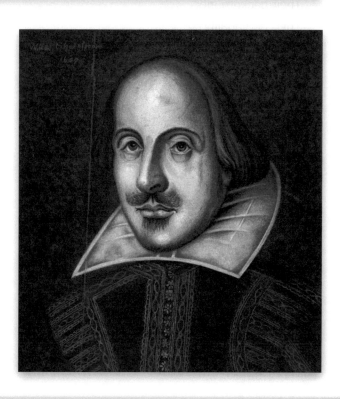

4A Shakespeare: Character

The Main Characters

You may get a question on a **character** from the Shakespeare play that you've studied. You need to be able to identify who the main characters are.

Think about which characters are important in the play you're studying. Why are they important? Are they main characters or minor characters who, nevertheless, impact greatly on the play? For example:

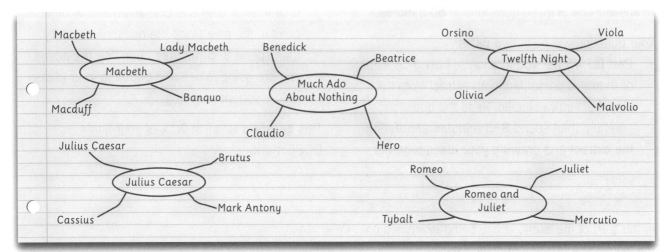

What the Main Characters are Like

You need to know what the main characters are like, how they behave and what their characteristics are. When examining what the characters are like, you should consider:

- Their background
- Their personality
- Their relationships with other characters
- Their motivation in the play.

For example:

Play	Character	Characteristics
Macbeth	Lady Macbeth	Ambitious, controlling, scheming, domineering
Much Ado About Nothing	Hero	Beautiful, innocent, friendly, gentle
Twelfth Night	Orsino	Obsessed, self-centred, determined, romantic
Julius Caesar	Mark Antony	Brave, intelligent, cunning, ambitious
Romeo and Juliet	Tybalt	Aggressive, unforgiving, arrogant, a trouble-maker

Proving Your Ideas with Quotations

It's important that you support your points with quotations from the text. You should look at what the character says and how they behave. You should also consider **what other characters think about them** from what they say about them or to them. For example:

- Lady Macbeth is domineering, 'Shame itself! Why do you make such faces? When all's done, you look but on a stool.'

- Hero is beautiful, 'Can the world buy such a jewel?'
- Orsino is obsessed, 'If music be the food of love, play on, give me excess of it.'
- Mark Antony is cunning, 'I doubt not of your wisdom. Let each man render me his bloody hand. First, Marcus Brutus, will I shake with you.'
- Tybalt is aggressive, 'Now by the stock and honour of my kin, to strike him dead I hold it not a sin.'

Analysing Your Quotations

You need to be able to comment on the **effect of specific words** in your quotations, for example:

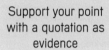

State your idea, or point, clearly

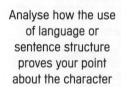

Support your point with a quotation as evidence

Analyse how the use of language or sentence structure proves your point about the character

Further analysis

Macbeth

Lady Macbeth is domineering, 'Shame itself! Why do you make such faces? When all's done, you look but on a stool.' The short sentences, exclamation and rhetorical question make her sound like she is telling Macbeth off. This is emphasised by the word 'shame', and the way the last sentence makes him sound foolish.

Much Ado About Nothing

Hero is beautiful, 'Can the world buy such a jewel?' Shakespeare uses this metaphor to show that Claudio is impressed by Hero. The word 'jewel' makes her sound perfect and special.

Twelfth Night

Orsino is obsessed, 'If music be the food of love, play on, give me excess of it.' The use of two verbs, combined with the word 'excess' show that Orsino cannot get enough of love. This is emphasised by the extended metaphor linking food to love.

Julius Caesar

Mark Antony is cunning, 'I doubt not of your wisdom. Let each man render me his bloody hand. First, Marcus Brutus, will I shake with you.' Antony follows praise ('wisdom') with a criticism ('blood') to show his public and private feelings about the conspirators. Shaking their hands is symbolic of making a pact.

Romeo and Juliet

Tybalt is aggressive, 'Now by the stock and honour of my kin, to strike him dead I hold it not a sin.' The verb phrase 'strike him dead' sounds powerful. This is added to by his belief that there is nothing wrong with killing people, if it is standing up for your family.

Quick Test

1. Write down four or five words to describe each of the main characters in the play you're studying and find a quotation to support each of the characteristics that you wrote down.

2. Who do you think is the nicest character in the play you're studying and why?

3. Who do you think is the most dislikeable character in the play you're studying and why?

4. Who do you think is the most important character in the play you're studying and why?

4A Shakespeare: Character Development

How Main Characters Change

In Shakespeare's plays, **characters develop as the story progresses**. They may grow up, go through an important experience or be affected by an event or relationship. Make sure you know which characters change during the play and in what ways they change. For example:

- *Macbeth*
  Macbeth changes from being brave, respected and honourable, to being a frightened and hated murderer.
- *Much Ado About Nothing*
  Benedick changes from being unromantic and rude (particularly to Beatrice), to being heroic, romantic and in love with Beatrice.
- *Twelfth Night*
  Malvolio changes from being respectable, fun-hating and dislikeable, to being foolish, in love and pitiable.
- *Julius Caesar*
  Brutus changes from noble, respectful and trusted, to being naive and treacherous.
- *Romeo and Juliet*
  Juliet changes from being well-behaved, disliking the Montagues and disinterested in love, to going against her parents and falling in love with a Montague.

Selecting and Analysing Quotations

Think about how you would answer a question in the exam relating to how characters change in the Shakespeare play you're studying.

When selecting quotations, you should look at **dramatic moments or episodes** where the character plays a key part in **making decisions**,

Think about which other characters go through **significant changes** in the play you're studying. For example, Claudio in *Much Ado About Nothing* or Lady Macbeth. What causes these changes? How does Shakespeare convey the changes?

You might want to consider making a **character log** to keep track of how a character changes throughout the play. This example illustrates the events in the play that affect Macbeth:

Event	The Effect Caused
Macbeth meets the witches for the first time.	He starts thinking about the future and his ambition to become king.
He kills Duncan.	Macbeth becomes king. He is powerful and turns against his friend Banquo.
He sees Banquo's ghost.	He feels guilty and starts to act strangely.
Macbeth visits the witches again.	He is very insecure and is frightened of losing his crown. He becomes more ruthless.
Macduff and Macolm invade Scotland.	Macbeth thinks he's invincible. He is defiant and brave.

Remember to use **connectives** of **comparison**, **time or consequence** to show the examiner that you understand a character is changing.

conflict or emotional turmoil. You should also consider what other characters say about them.

You'll need to make **specific comments** on how Shakespeare uses a range of **language and stagecraft techniques** to reveal how a character changes.

Key Words   **Connective**

Selecting and Analysing Quotations (Cont.)

Macbeth

At the start of the play Macbeth is brave, 'For brave Macbeth (well he deserves that name), Disdaining Fortune, with his brandish'd steel, Which smok'd with bloody execution'. The captain's words show he is impressed with Macbeth's bravery. He emphasises his feelings with his comment in parenthesis. The use of metaphor shows he stopped at nothing to honour the King, and words like 'steel' and 'execution' show his strength and determination.

However, by Act 3, Macbeth seems scared by visions of guilt, 'Hence, horrible shadow! Unreal mock'ry, hence!' The adjectives show his terror of the unknown. The repetition of 'hence' also sounds scared, and this emotion is emphasised by the short sentences and exclamation marks to suggest shouting.

Twelfth Night

Early on in the play, Malvolio is a serious, prudish character, 'My masters, are you mad? Or what are you? Have you no wit, manners, nor honesty, but to gabble like tinkers at this time of night?' His three rhetorical questions show he is shocked and appalled by Sir Toby and Sir Andrew's drunkenness. The list of their missing virtues and his insulting simile show that he is telling the men off for their behaviour.

Later on, he is tricked into believing that Olivia loves him, Malvolio becomes more light-hearted and foolish, 'To bed? Ay, sweetheart, and I'll come to thee'. His mention of bed and the colloquial 'sweetheart' show he is being flirtatious. The fact that he is quoting a popular song from Shakespeare's time also makes him sound less serious.

Much Ado About Nothing

Benedick doesn't seem at all romantic at the start of the play, 'But I hope you have no intent to turn husband, have you? [...] Is't come to this?' The phrase 'turn husband' makes getting married sound like a crime. In addition, his questions (especially the second one) come across as despairing of Claudio's romance.

However, as the play progresses, Benedick falls in love with Beatrice and he ends the play saying, 'Prince, thou art sad; get thee a wife, get thee a wife!' He has completely changed his views, and we see him using an imperative to urge Don Pedro to get married. This dramatic shift is emphasised by the repetition and exclamation mark.

Use a connective phrase to establish your first point

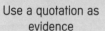

Use a quotation as evidence

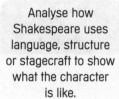

Analyse how Shakespeare uses language, structure or stagecraft to show what the character is like.

Develop your analysis further

Use a connective phrase to establish your next point and show character development

Quick Test

1. Find quotations that show how a character in the play you've studied has changed.
2. Do the characters in the play that you've studied change for better or worse? Why?
3. What different things in the play that you've studied cause people to change?

4A Shakespeare: Setting and Context

Setting

It's important that you're aware of the setting of the Shakespeare play you've studied. This means examining both when and where the play is set, for example:

Play	Setting
Macbeth	11th century Scotland
Much Ado About Nothing	16th century Messina (a port of Sicily)
Twelfth Night	16th century Illyria (on the eastern coast of the Adriatic Sea)
Julius Caesar	44BC Rome, Italy
Romeo and Juliet	14th/15th century Verona, Italy

For the play that you've studied, think about anything in the play that **links to the setting**. For example, in *Twelfth Night*, Viola and Sebastian are shipwrecked so the setting has to be on a coast.

Context

When you consider the context of a play, you need to look at the **society** and the **historical events** that appear in, or link to, it. Shakespeare often drew on existing stories and real life events in his plays. It's important to consider the **assumptions**, **beliefs and manners** of the audience at the time when Shakespeare wrote his plays. For example:

- *Macbeth*
  The divine right of kingship; James I's interest in the supernatural.
- *Much Ado About Nothing*
  'Courtly' behaviour; **traditional expectations** of women; attitudes towards illegitimacy.

- *Twelfth Night*
  'Courtly' behaviour; the festival of 'Twelfth Night' where those at the bottom of the social scale change places with those at the top.
- *Julius Caesar*
  The historical assassination of Julius Caesar in 44BC; Roman politics.
- *Romeo and Juliet*
  14th/15th century upper class expectations of women, children and marriage.

Why Settings and Context Affect the Play

In the exam, you need to comment on how the play's **setting and context affects the characters or the events** in the play. For example:

- The divine right of kings is important in *Macbeth*. Not only has Macbeth murdered someone very important, but he has murdered someone chosen by God. The consequences aren't just criminal, they are religious as he believes he will now go to Hell.

Why Settings and Context Affect the Play (Cont.)

- Traditional expectations of women are important in *Much Ado About Nothing*. The play is a comedy and part of the humour comes from the fact that Beatrice doesn't behave like the other women in the play (such as Hero).
- In *Twelfth Night*, the traditional festival of chaos is being used to create humour by inspiring all the disguises, mistakes and confusion.
- *Julius Caesar* is a historical play, which is based on the actual assassination of the Roman dictator. Shakespeare is also using the political intrigue to make the play more interesting.
- Traditional expectations of women and children are important in *Romeo and Juliet* because they help us to judge how Juliet is treated by her parents.

Think about how the other **contextual elements** of your play are important. For example, in *Much Ado About Nothing*, how might the way Don John is treated over his illegitimacy affect his character?

Analysing Setting and Context

You should try to build in **comments on the setting or context into your analysis**. Don't just write about it for the sake of it, but include it if it's relevant as you'll get extra marks. For example:

Relevance of the context in understanding character

> Romeo and Juliet
>
> At the start of the play, Lord Capulet comes across as quite a modern father who has respect for his daughter's opinions, 'My will to her consent is but a part'. When talking of Paris's marriage proposal, Shakespeare uses the word 'consent' to show that Capulet considers the final decision to be Juliet's, which was unusual for a time when girls were married off to whichever suitor their father preferred.
>
> After the death of Tybalt, Lord Capulet becomes a much stricter father and follows the traditional conventions of marriage, 'go with Paris to Saint Peter's Church, Or I will drag thee on a hurdle thither.' The use of threat and the verb 'drag', show he is now speaking about Juliet as if she is his possession, rather than an individual with choices.
>
> His threatening manner and references to possession continue when he says, 'And you be mine I'll give you to my friend; And you be not, hang! Beg! Starve! Die in the streets!' The possessive pronoun (mine) and the verb 'give' link to marriage as a transaction. The consequences of being disowned (made frightening by the short sentences and exclamation marks) would have been very real for a girl in the time the play was set, as women had no rights or social security.

Quick Test

1. What quotations can you find and analyse that link to the setting or context of the play you've studied?
2. Which characters in the play you've studied are affected by the setting or context and in what ways?
3. What events in the play you've studied are affected by the setting or context and in what ways?

4A Shakespeare: Themes

The Themes of the Play

In the exam, you might be asked **how Shakespeare presents a theme and develops it during the play**.

So, to start with, you need to be able to identify what the themes are in the play you're studying, for example:

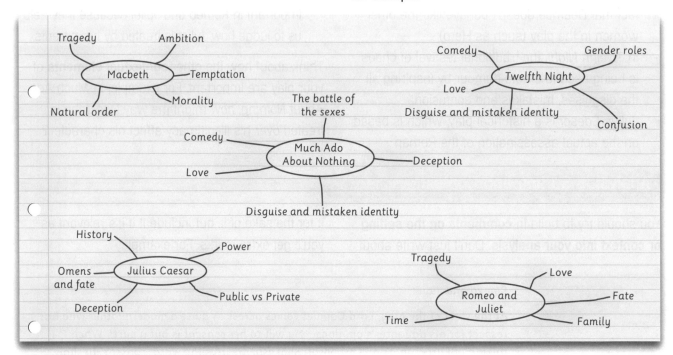

Where the Themes Appear

In order to explore how a theme is developed, **you need to know where it appears** in the play.

Shakespeare presents the themes of his plays through **dialogue and action**. You should also keep in mind that the plays were written to be performed and sometimes **visual images** can indicate a lot about the issues and ideas in the play.

- *Macbeth*
  Ambition is shown through the characters of Macbeth and Lady Macbeth. The witches play on Macbeth's ambitions, and his wife pushes him on because of her own ambitions. Macbeth has to continue killing to sustain his ambitions.
- *Much Ado About Nothing*
  Deception is shown through Don John's tricking of Claudio, the tricks that Don Pedro plays on Beatrice and Benedick, and Hero's final test of Claudio.

- *Twelfth Night*
  Many different types of love appear: Orsino's obsessive love for Olivia; Malvolio's foolish love for Olivia and for himself; the romantic love triangle of Olivia, Cesario/Viola, and Orsino.
- *Julius Caesar*
  Omens appear to Caesar in the form of the soothsayer's warning, Calpurnia's dream and the sacrificial animal. Other omens are witnessed by Casca, Cassius and Brutus.
- *Romeo and Juliet*
  Time is a recurring problem, from the short deadline for Juliet to marry Paris, to the mis-timing of the Friar's note to Romeo. The story only takes place over about five days, bringing a feeling of time quickly running out for the lovers.

Analysing How Quotations Show a Theme

If you're asked about themes in the exam, you need to be able to **support your answer with suitable quotations**. You need to select quotations and **analyse how that theme is presented through Shakespeare's choices of language and structure**, for example:

> ### Macbeth
>
> Lady Macbeth is used to explore ambition at the start of the play when she says of her husband: 'Thou wouldst be great; Art not without ambition, but without The illness should attend it.' This shows that both characters are 'ambitious and excited by greatness. But she also suggests that to be successfully ambitious, you also need to be cruel ('illness').
>
> This idea is developed later in the play when she accuses Macbeth of letting fear get in the way of ambition, 'Art thou afeard To be the same in thine own act and valour, As thou art in desire?' She doesn't see Macbeth's doubts as morality but cowardice, and uses the rhetorical question to mock his weakness.
>
> ### Julius Caesar
>
> Omens are presented in the play as things not to be ignored. Caesar does this repeatedly and is assassinated at the start of Act 3. The first instance of this is when the soothsayer warns him to beware the Ides of March (a statement then symbolically repeated by Brutus), and he responds, 'He is a dreamer. Let us leave him. Pass'. The short sentences show Caesar is completely dismissing the omen.
>
> This happens again when he ignores Calpurnia's dream. She says, 'Your wisdom is consumed in confidence. Do not go forth today'. The metaphor suggests that it is sensible to listen to omens, and her anxious imperative shows that she believes they are accurate.

Opening point about a theme

↓

Evidence

↓

Analysis of the quotation relating to the theme

Connective phrase to develop your ideas

Quick Test

1. What do you think is the most important theme in the play you've studied and why do you think this?
2. Which events in the play you've studied link to different themes? In what ways?
3. Which characters in the play you've studied link to different themes? In what ways?
4. Find and analyse quotations that link to the themes of the play you've studied.

Language Techniques

In your **analysis of Shakespeare**, you should always comment on the **effect of his choice of words and images**. You should also look out for, and comment on, any **language techniques** that Shakespeare uses.

Language Technique	Description	Examples from Shakespeare's Plays
Dramatic Irony	Dramatic irony is when the audience know something important that one of the characters doesn't.	In *Julius Caesar*, the ignored warnings of Calpurnia and the soothsayer have more dramatic impact because we know that Caesar is going to die. Shakespeare does a similar thing in *Romeo and Juliet* when, in the Prologue, he tells us Romeo and Juliet are doomed.
Foreshadowing	Linking to dramatic irony, Shakespeare often includes images or references to things that are going to happen.	In *Romeo and Juliet*, Juliet's line from Act 3 scene 5, "Methinks I see thee, now thou art so low, As one dead in the bottom of a tomb", foreshadows the lovers' final scene.
Wordplay	Wordplay is where characters use words that have double-meanings, or that sound like other words, in order to create a joke or to add an extra layer of meaning to what is being said.	At the start of *Twelfth Night*, the use of the word 'hart' (which is a deer, but sounds like 'heart'), is used to joke about trying to catch the one you love.
Innuendo	Innuendo is a phrase which implies a secondary meaning, usually sexual.	In Act 2 scene 3 of *Much Ado About Nothing*, Leonato says of a letter, 'she found 'Benedick' and 'Beatrice' between the sheet'. 'Sheet' refers to a piece of paper, but is also used to mean bed sheet to suggest the two characters are attracted to each other.
Verse / Prose	Characters' lines are sometimes written by Shakespeare in verse (like poetry) and sometimes in prose (like a novel).	As a generalisation, characters of a high class are usually given verse, compared to characters of a low class being given prose; but this doesn't happen all the time. Verse is also used to heighten emotions, such as the sonnet that Romeo and Juliet share when they first meet in Act 1 scene 5.

Stagecraft

It's important to remember that you've been **studying a play**, so you should think about **how it would look on stage**. The examiner doesn't want you to write about what you think it should look like, but you should **comment on anything Shakespeare has deliberately included that affects what we see**.

Soliloquy

A **soliloquy** is when a **character speaks their thoughts when alone on stage or as an aside** so other characters cannot hear. Soliloquies are very important in revealing to the audience a character's true feelings, and gives an extra insight into their characteristics. For example, look at the soliloquy by Cassius in *Julius Caesar* at the end of Act 1 scene 2.

Interruption

Characters often **interrupt** each other to give **more impact to arguments** or to **show the dominance of a character**. Shakespeare uses **punctuation** to show this by adding a dash at the end of someone's speech, or by two characters sharing the ten syllables given to a line of verse. For example, we can see this in Act 3 scene 4, where Lady Macbeth doesn't believe that Macbeth has seen the ghost of Banquo:

Macb.	If I stand here, I saw him.
Lady M.	Fie, for shame!

Disguise and Masks

Disguise and masks can be used to **create passion and excitement** (such as the masque scene in *Romeo and Juliet*), or to **create comedy** (as with the mistaken identities in *Twelfth Night*).

Concealment

Concealment is when a character on stage hides from others, either for **serious or comedic impact**. For example, the trick that Ursula and Hero play on Beatrice in Act 3 scene 1 of *Much Ado About Nothing*.

Weather

Many writers and playwrights use weather to reflect characters' feelings and dramatic events. **Thunder and lightning** are used several times by Shakespeare **to suggest danger or evil**. For example, when the witches are introduced in *Macbeth*, or in the opening of Act 1 scene 3 of *Julius Caesar* (straight after Cassius's treacherous soliloquy).

Quick Test

1. Which language technique do you think has most impact in the play you've studied?
2. What is the most effective use of stagecraft in the play you've studied?
3. Choose one character from the play you've studied. How is what we know and think about them affected by language techniques and stagecraft?

Understanding the Question

In your exam, your question about a Shakespeare play may read something like this:

> **(a)** How is Banquo presented in this extract from Act 1 scene 3 of *Macbeth*?
>
> **(b)** How is Banquo presented in another part of the play?

You need to **read the question carefully** and note the **key words or phrases**. For example:

- <u>How</u> and <u>presented</u>: The examiner doesn't want you to just describe the play. You're expected to **pick out quotations** and say how **specific words, punctuation or techniques** are being used to show things to the reader.

- <u>Banquo</u>: In the exam, you'll usually get the **choice of a question on a character** (or a relationship between two characters) and a **question on a theme**. **Keep focussed** on the essay question so that everything you write is **relevant**.

- <u>Act 1 scene 3</u> and <u>another part of the play</u>: In the first part of the question, **make sure you only comment on the extract**. In the second part of the question, you'll need to **choose another part of the play to explore**; only comment on the section you choose (not things from throughout the play).

Making Your Plan

For **part (a)**, you should **spend 3–5 minutes annotating the extract** and working out **what it tells you about the theme or character** you've been asked to focus on. Once you've done this, quickly **number your ideas into a logical order** and **spend 20–25 minutes writing**.

For **part (b)**, quickly **choose the part of the play** you're going to explore and plan how it **relates to the theme or character** that you're focussing on. **Spend about 3–5 minutes** doing this, then **number your ideas in a logical order** and get writing, for example:

> (b) <u>Banquo in Act 3 scene 1</u>
> - Suspicious of how Macbeth became king (lines 1–3). ②
> - Also ambitious regarding the witches' prophecies (lines 3–10). ⑤
> - Respectful to the new king (lines 15–17). ①
> - Unaware of the danger he is in (lines 20–27; 35–36). ⑥
> - Feared and respected by Macbeth (lines 48–56). ③
> - Macbeth sees Banquo as equally ambitious (lines 55–59). ④

Answering the Question

For **both sections**, you need to **follow your plan** and try to **use a clear structure**, for example, PEA.

It's important that you **choose your quotations carefully** so that they *allow* you **detailed analysis**; if you choose a boring quotation (without any interesting words, punctuation or techniques) you'll find it hard to say anything about it.

Remember, you shouldn't **compare the extract and the other part of the play that you choose**. This will take you a lot longer and doesn't get you any extra marks.

What to Expect in the Exam

In **Unit 4, Section B** you'll be given a **choice of two questions** on the novel that you've studied. You'll need to answer one of these questions in **40 minutes**; you should read the question carefully, then spend **3–5 minutes planning your ideas** before you begin writing.

This **question** is worth 15% of your final GCSE mark.

If you're doing the **foundation paper**, the question will be split into **two parts** to help you:

- **Part (a)** will ask you to analyse the presentation of a character or theme.
- **Part (b)** will ask you to comment on how the same character or theme relates to the context of the novel.

If you're taking the **higher** paper, the question will not be split into two parts.

How the Exam is Assessed

In this part of the exam, you're being examined on the following assessment objectives:

AO1	Respond to texts critically and imaginatively; select and evaluate relevant textual detail to illustrate and support interpretations.	33.3% of this question
AO2	Explain how language, structure and form contribute to writers' presentation of ideas, themes and settings.	33.3% of this question
AO4	Relate texts to their social, cultural and historical contexts; explain how texts have been influential and significant to self and other readers in different contexts and at different times.	33.3% of this question

Understanding Your Text

Whichever text from the English Literary Heritage you are studying, you'll need to have a good understanding of:

- **Characters**: who the main characters are, how they act and why.
- **Setting**: where and when the text is set and its effect on the characters and their lives.
- **Context**: how the text relates to its social, historical and cultural context.
- **Themes**: how ideas and issues are explored in the story and portrayed to the reader.
- **Language, structure and form**: how the writer uses these techniques to get their ideas across.

4B The ELH: Character

The Main Characters

As with the other parts of the exam, you may get a question on a character from the text that you've studied.

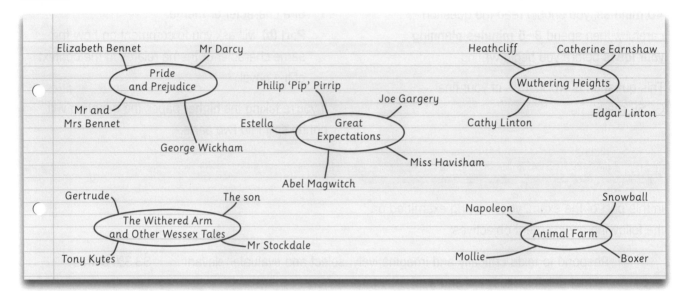

What the Main Characters are Like

Once you know who the main characters are, you need to consider the following:
- What they are like
- What they do
- How they fit into society
- Their function in the text.

Try to think of four or five words that describe each of the main characters in the text you're studying.

Text	Character	Characteristics
Pride and Prejudice	Elizabeth Bennet	Clever, witty and attractive but tends to judge people too quickly.
Wuthering Heights	Heathcliff	Mysterious, romantic, powerful and vengeful.
Great Expectations	Joe Gargery	Kind, hard-working and forgiving but could also be seen as weak.
The Withered Arm and Other Wessex Tales	Mr Stockdale	Religious, serious, likeable, lonely, honest but naive.
Animal Farm	Boxer	Loyal, hard-working, respected and kind but impressionable.

Proving Your Ideas with Quotations

You need to provide evidence of what the characters are like by using quotations. These can be descriptions or speech (said by, or about, the character), for example:
- Elizabeth Bennet is clever, 'they are all silly and ignorant like other girls; but Lizzy has something more of quickness than her sisters'.

- Heathcliff is powerful, 'What *can* you mean by talking in this way to *me*?' thundered Heathcliff with savage vehemence'.
- Joe is kind, 'We don't know what you have done, but we wouldn't have you starved to death for it, poor miserable fellow-creature'.

Proving Your Ideas with Quotations (Cont.)

- Mr Stockdale is lonely, 'a lonely young fellow, who had for weeks felt a great craving for somebody on whom to throw away superfluous interest, and even tenderness'.

- Boxer is impressionable, 'Napoleon is always right'.

Analysing Your Quotations

You also need to be able to comment on the **effect of specific words in your quotations**, for example:

State your idea, or point, clearly

↓

Support your idea with a quotation as evidence

↓

Analyse how the use of language or sentence structure proves your point about the character

↓

Further analysis

Pride and Prejudice

Elizabeth Bennet is clever, 'they are all silly and ignorant like other girls; but Lizzy has something more of quickness than her sisters'. Mr Bennet's comparison of his other daughters to Elizabeth, and his use of the adjective 'quickness', shows he is impressed by her intelligence.

Wuthering Heights

Heathcliff is powerful, 'What can you mean by talking in this way to me?' thundered Heathcliff with savage vehemence'. The descriptions of Heathcliff's speech ('thundered', 'savage vehemence') make him sound frightening. The italics give extra emphasis to the word 'me', showing that he knows he is powerful.

Great Expectations

Joe is kind, 'We don't know what you have done, but we wouldn't have you starved to death for it, poor miserable fellow-creature'. Joe doesn't judge Magwitch ('we don't know'), and wants him to be treated well. His adjectives show sympathy for Magwitch and this is emphasised by the phrase 'fellow-creature'.

The Withered Arm and Other Wessex Tales

Mr Stockdale is lonely, 'a lonely young fellow, who had for weeks felt a great craving for somebody on whom to throw away superfluous interest, and even tenderness'. As well as the adjective 'lonely', the phrase 'great craving' shows us that he wants somebody to talk to or care for.

Animal Farm

Boxer is impressionable, 'Napoleon is always right'. Boxer repeats this phrase, despite the obvious corruption. The use of the intensifier 'always' shows how much Boxer has been taken in by the pigs.

Quick Test

1. Who is the most interesting character in the text you've studied? Why?
2. Which character do you feel most sorry for? Why do you feel sorry for them?
3. Who do you think is the nicest or the most dislikeable character? Why?

How Main Characters Change

Throughout the text that you've studied, you'll discover that **characters can change during the story**. You may be asked a question on this in the exam so it's important that you know which main characters change.

It might be a good idea to keep a **character log** (see page 54) so that you can keep track of how characters change in the text you've studied:

- Look at passages from different parts of the text where a character plays a key part.
- Ensure these passages reflect the way the character develops.
- Look at descriptive passages and dramatic moments.

Start with one character from the text and explore how they change through the story, for example:

- *Pride and Prejudice*
  Mr Wickham seems honourable, charming and romantic, but proves himself to be selfish, untrustworthy, nasty and immoral.

- *Wuthering Heights*
  As a young man, Edgar Linton is well-bred but spoiled. However, he matures into a kind and reliable, although rather cowardly, gentleman.
- *Great Expectations*
  Miss Havisham is mad, cruel and obsessive, but eventually feels guilt for what she does.
- *The Withered Arm and Other Wessex Tales*
  Phyllis, in *The Melancholy Hussar*, feels trapped and miserable, but gains love and hope, only to be left disappointed and distraught.
- *Animal Farm*
  Napoleon begins as a quiet and stubborn character but becomes increasingly violent, deceptive, selfish and hypocritical.

Think about other characters in the text you've studied that go through **significant changes**. For example, Pip in *Great Expectations* or Rhoda in *The Withered Arm*. How do characters' relationships with others change through the text? Do they develop new relationships?

Selecting and Analysing Quotations

To prove your point, it's important to find quotations and make specific comments on how the words and punctuation in your quotations show changing **characteristics**. Remember to use connectives in your response, for example:

Use a connective phrase to establish your first point

⬇

Support your idea with a quotation as evidence

⬇

Analyse how language and structure are used to show character

Use a connective phrase to establish your next point

Pride and Prejudice

Early on in the novel, Mr Wickham seems very charming, 'with ready delight was he received at the other table between Elizabeth and Lydia… Mr Wickham was therefore at leisure to talk to Elizabeth, and she was very willing to hear him'. The word 'delight' shows that women find Mr Wickham attractive, with Elizabeth's enjoyment at the conversation emphasising his charm.

However, we soon realise that Mr Wickham's charms are all put on, 'She had even learnt to detect, in the very gentleness which had first delighted her, an affectation and a sameness to disgust and weary'. The word 'affectation' shows that Wickham is false (only paying Elizabeth attention again, now that, richer, Mary King has left town), and opposites ('delighted' and 'disgust') are used to show how Elizabeth can now see through him.

Great Expectations

We realise that Miss Havisham is a cruel and manipulative character, 'with a searching glance that seemed to pry into my heart and probe its wounds. 'How does she use you Pip; how does she use you?' she asked me again with her witch-like eagerness'. The 'eagerness' with which Miss Havisham discovers Pip's broken heart is horrible, with her repeated questions showing her enjoyment of Pip's misery. This is emphasised by the comparison of her to a witch.

Towards the end of the novel, though, Miss Havisham regrets her behaviour, ''O!' she cried, despairingly. 'What have I done! What have I done!''. The monosyllabic exclamation and the adverb show her guilt, and this is emphasised by her repeated phrases. The choice of exclamation marks, rather than a question mark, shows that she knows exactly the terrible things she is guilty of.

Quick Test

1. In the book you've studied, which character undergoes the biggest change? How do they change?
2. Do the characters in the book that you've studied change for better or worse? Why?
3. What different things in the book that you've studied cause people to change?

4B The ELH: Setting and Context

Setting

It's important that you're aware of not only **when the text is set**, but also **where it is set**. For example:

Text	Setting
Pride and Prejudice	19th century southern England
Wuthering Heights	Late-18th century Yorkshire, England
Great Expectations	Mid-19th century London and the surrounding countryside
The Withered Arm and Other Wessex Tales	19th century, south-west England
Animal Farm	Mid-20th century, England

Context

When we consider the **context** of a book, we look at the **society** and the **historical events** that appear in, or link to, the story. For example:

- *Pride and Prejudice*
  The landed gentry's values and beliefs about things like **gender**, marriage, **morality** and behaviour.
- *Wuthering Heights*
  When the book was published in 1847, people thought it was too brutal and passionate. The '**Victorian values**' of the time also meant there were strict social codes of conduct.
- *Great Expectations*
  The contrast between the different social **classes** of the mid-1800s. London was growing as an industrial city whilst the countryside was comparatively poor and isolated.
- *The Withered Arm and Other Wessex Tales*
  How different classes or occupations viewed marriage, gender and morality.
- *Animal Farm*
  Published in 1945, the book is an **allegory**, and reflects the events in Russia that led up to World War Two.

Why Settings and Context Affect the Text

You need to be able to **comment on how the setting and context affects the characters or events in the text**. For example:

- The landed gentry's views of marriage and morality are important in *Pride and Prejudice*, helping us to understand the reaction to Lydia and Mr Wickham eloping together.
- 19th century views on what could be written about are vital to understanding how passionate the relationship between Catherine and Heathcliff is in *Wuthering Heights*, whilst social codes help to explain why she doesn't feel she can marry him.
- In *Great Expectations*, the difference between life in London and in the countryside help to emphasise how Pip changes and becomes distant from Joe.
- Expectations of women's roles in the 19th century help us to understand why women behave as they do in *Tony Kytes Arch Deceiver*, as well as allowing us to explore its use of (what we'd now see as quite sexist) comedy.
- The events of Stalinist Russia allow us to explore the characters and events of *Animal Farm* as an allegory, rather than simply as a 'fairy tale'.

Think about the other contextual elements and why they are important. For example, you could consider how the **views of different social classes** affect the characters in *The Son's Veto*.

Analysing Setting and Context

You should try to include comments on the **setting or context in your analysis**. For example:

> Great Expectations
>
> In chapter 27, we can see the development of Pip and Joe's relationship. Joe clearly wants to live up to Pip's new social status, saying: 'Pip, how AIR you, Pip?' Dickens spells 'are' differently to show that Joe is trying – because of his uneducated background – to put on a higher class accent so as not to cause embarrassment. The way it is written also shows us that Joe fails, as he sounds over the top.
>
> We also see that Joe is intimidated by Pip's new social status, 'I presented Joe to Herbert, who held out his hand; but Joe backed from it, and held on by the bird's nest.' The handshake is a symbol of social conventions and Joe clearly doesn't know what to do. Instead, again symbolically, he clings on to his own symbol of status (his hat). We can see the change in Pip and Joe's relationship by the way Dickens uses the mocking 'bird's nest' metaphor to describe the two men's different impressions of the hat.
>
> Joe refers to his clothes again when he discusses the difficulty of moving between social classes, 'I'm wrong in these clothes. I'm wrong out of the forge, the kitchen, or off th'meshes.' The short sentence, repetition and use of a list emphasise how Joe now feels out of place around Pip. This is added to by his use of slang at the end, contrasting with Pip's grammatically correct speech throughout the chapter.

Reference to how the context tells us something about the character

Quick Test

1. Which characters in the book you've studied are affected by the setting or context? In what ways are they affected?
2. What events in the book you've studied are affected by the setting or context? In what ways are they affected?

Key Words   Accent • Symbol • Social conventions

The Themes of the Book

Often writers examine **various** themes in their stories. For example, **attitudes to money, society and class**, **marriage** and **social conventions**.

Remember that some of the **attitudes and ideas** expressed in the texts from the English Literary Heritage may differ from those you might expect today.

Identify what the main themes are in the text you've studied, for example:

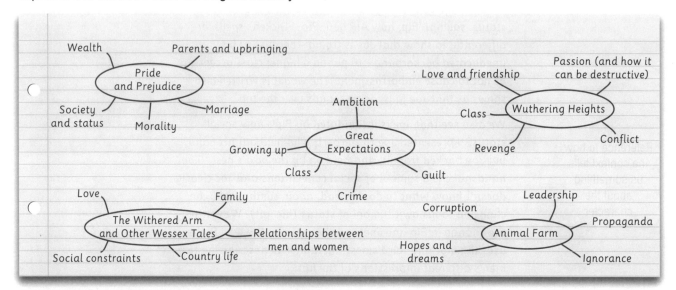

Where the Themes Appear

A **theme can often be developed** through **characters** or **events**, for example:

- *Pride and Prejudice*
  Parenting and upbringing is shown through Mr and Mrs Bennet. She's too focused on social climbing, whilst he makes fun of his younger daughters. In the novel, it's suggested that Mr and Mrs Bennet are to blame for Lydia's behaviour. This theme can also be explored in how Mr Darcy's upbringing shaped his character.
- *Wuthering Heights*
  Conflict appears between characters, most obviously Heathcliff and Edgar. It can also be seen within characters, such as Catherine's difficulty in choosing between the two men and between the two realms of nature and culture.

- *Great Expectations*
  Crime is presented mostly through the characters of Magwitch and Jaggers. However, characters like Pip are used to explore attitudes to crime; his own feelings of morality force him to question the law when Magwitch returns.
- *The Withered Arm and Other Wessex Tales*
  Relationships between men and women are explored in tales like *Tony Kytes* (his inability to choose between three women), *The Withered Arm* (the triangle of Rhoda, Farmer Lodge and Gertrude), and *The Distracted Preacher* (Mr Stockdale and Lizzy).
- *Animal Farm*
  Most of the animals on the farm seem ignorant of the pigs' corruption. With no written documents, their memories of the past are easily manipulated. Boxer is the best example of the dangers of ignorance, particularly in his last scene.

Analysing How Quotations Illustrate a Theme

Once you know where the themes appear in your book, you need to **select quotations** and **analyse how a theme is presented** through the **author's language choices**.

You need to try to comment on what is being said about a theme. For example:

Opening point to introduce theme

Analysis of how language is used to explore the theme

Development of idea about the theme

Analysis of language and structure

Wuthering Heights

In 'Wuthering Heights', conflict is presented through the characters of Heathcliff and Edgar Linton. When they first meet, 'Heathcliff's violent nature was not prepared to endure the appearance of impertinence from one whom he seemed to hate, even then, as a rival.' The word 'rival' shows us conflict between the two boys, and the 'impertinence' suggests it is based on Heathcliff's feelings of superiority (in the face of Edgar's actual social superiority). The phrase 'even then' signals to the reader that this conflict is set to grow.

Their conflict is clearly linked to love and class. Catherine tries to keep them apart because, 'when Heathcliff expressed contempt of Linton, in his presence, she could not half coincide, as she did in his absence; and when Linton evinced disgust and antipathy to Heathcliff...' The sentence structure establishes the two men as opposites. The phrase 'disgust and antipathy' suggests Linton looks down on Heathcliff, seeing him as almost worthless. This fuels the other's 'contempt', and so he tries to put him down around Catherine.

Quotation providing evidence

Evidence

Quick Test

1. What do you think is the most important theme in the book you've studied? Why do you think this?
2. Which events link to different themes? In what ways?
3. Which characters link to different themes? How are they linked?

4B The ELH: Characteristic Style

Style and Influence

As part of your study of the English Literary Heritage, you'll have read a book by a great author. Examiners want you to understand **what stands out** about that author's style of writing: their **choices of language, structure and form**. This is what we mean by **characteristic style**.

The Author's Style

When examining the author's style, you should look at and think about:

- **Genre**: What kind of text is it? Romance, tragedy, etc.
- **Narrative structure**: Is the text in a straightforward chronological order? What effect does the structure have on the text and the reader?

- **Narrative style**: Who is the narrator? Is it the main character or the author? Think about why the author uses a particular style. What effect does this have on the reader?
- **Language**: What kind of tone does the narrator use? What does the way the characters speak tell the reader about them? Think about the language techniques used to create mood and atmosphere.

Pride and Prejudice

- *Pride and Prejudice* is written in the **third person** (what is sometimes called indirect speech). However, as in many of her novels, Jane Austen also mixes in free indirect speech: so some of the narrative seems to come from the point of view of the characters (even though it isn't in the **first person**). This free indirect speech is usually used around Elizabeth, allowing the reader to get to know her better and slanting the narrative so we share her thoughts (and sometimes prejudices).

- The novel is also notable for the amount of **dialogue** that it contains, rather than description. This focuses the reader on the characters' thoughts and behaviour, making them seem more real. She often includes short sentences, questions and quick replies to build up the relationship between characters (such as the witty banter between Elizabeth and Darcy).

Wuthering Heights

- *Wuthering Heights* is immediately striking because of its complex narrative structure. The story is Lockwood's diary of what Nelly tells him about Wuthering Heights. So we get two different **narrative forms** and voices, both of which are quite **conventional** compared to the unconventional storyline.

- Emily Brontë's writing stands out as being quite different from other novelists of the time. Her language is very poetic, drawing on nature, but also very gothic with lots of dark, almost supernatural, descriptions.

Key Words   Third person • First person • Dialogue • Narrative form • Conventional

The Author's Style (Cont.)

Great Expectations

- *Great Expectations* is written in the first person; a popular way of writing at the time, which follows the personal development of an individual (also known as a 'bildungsroman').
- Typically for Charles Dickens, the storyline is complex and contains a number of entangled relationships and coincidences. We meet lots of characters who are described in great detail.

- When doing this, Dickens often uses comparisons with inanimate objects (possibly to show a lack of **empathy** from Pip).
- Dickens also uses lots of deliberate misspellings and grammatical errors to convey characters' speech, for example to mirror Joe's accent and lack of education.

The Withered Arm and Other Wessex Tales

- Thomas Hardy's writing is often described as **Naturalism**, a style which was quite new when he was writing. Descriptions are detailed and photographic in their realism, in order to show that people's behaviour is shaped by their environment, social conditions and family background.

- Hardy's characters are often everyday, country people placed in unusual situations. Deliberate misspellings and grammatical errors are often used to convey their **rural** speech. Some of Hardy's storylines also cover issues that were **taboo** at the time, such as illegitimate children. These things made the stories unusual and popular when they were published.

Animal Farm

- George Orwell deliberately uses a very simple style of writing in this book, with short sentences, quite basic vocabulary and a matter-of-fact tone. This is done to express his ideas as clearly as possible, in contrast to the vagueness of the manipulating pigs (and the type of human being they represent). Sometimes this simplicity of writing makes chapters more dramatic because they seem more brutal.
- The story is an **allegory**, with lots of characters and events representing different aspects of life in Russia under Stalin's communist regime. For example, at the very start, Old Major's dream can be seen as an allegory of Karl Marx's communist manifesto. Orwell is **satirising** politics and politicians.

- The story is also written as a fable, or a fairy story, rather than a history essay. This means that we make our own links to politics and history, without simply being told them, which gives the meaning greater impact.

Quick Test

1. Can you find particular passages, and quotations, that show the typical style of the book that you've studied?
2. How does the style of writing affect your response to the characters in the book you've studied?
3. How does the style of writing affect your responses to the events of the book you've studied?

Key Words   Empathy • Naturalism • Rural • Taboo • Allegory • Satire

4B The ELH: Approaching the Question

Understanding the Question

Your question may read something like this:

> How does Dickens present the ways in which Pip changes when he moves to London? How does this reflect the society into which he moves?

You need to **read the question carefully** and note the **key words or phrases**. For example:

- How and present: You're expected to **pick out quotations** and say how **specific words,**

punctuation or techniques are being used to show things to the reader.

- Pip changes: You'll usually get the choice of a **question on a character** (or a relationship between two characters) and a **question on a theme**. **Keep focussed on the essay question** so that everything you write is relevant.
- Reflect the society: Link the text back to its **historical or cultural context**: how people lived or behaved because of **the time, the place, and their position in society**.

Planning Your Answer

Spend five minutes planning your ideas. You could note down any **important page references** that you'll need when you come to use quotations.

Think about the **novel's context** and how this links to the question you've been set. You should try to give **your plan a logical order** so you write an essay that **flows in a clear and sensible way**.

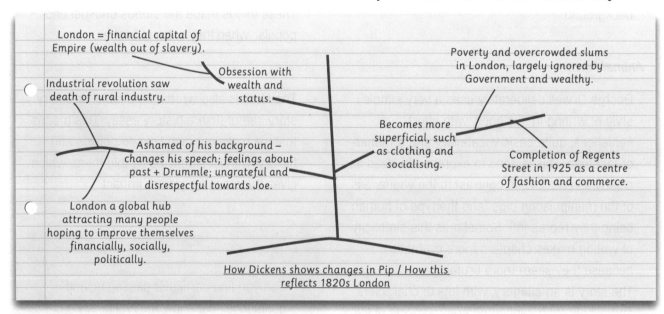

London = financial capital of Empire (wealth out of slavery).

Industrial revolution saw death of rural industry.

Obsession with wealth and status.

Ashamed of his background – changes his speech; feelings about past + Drummle; ungrateful and disrespectful towards Joe.

London a global hub attracting many people hoping to improve themselves financially, socially, politically.

Poverty and overcrowded slums in London, largely ignored by Government and wealthy.

Becomes more superficial, such as clothing and socialising.

Completion of Regents Street in 1925 as a centre of fashion and commerce.

How Dickens shows changes in Pip / How this reflects 1820s London

Answering the Question

Follow your plan and try to use a **clear structure**, for example, PEA.

Remember, **choose your quotations carefully** so that they *allow* you detailed analysis: if you choose a boring quotation (without any interesting words,

punctuation or techniques) you'll find it hard to say anything about it.

If you've learned some quotations, that's great. However, **only use quotations that you've learned if they're relevant to the essay title**.

Unit 4 Section A

Macbeth

Foundation

Part (a) How does the following extract from Act 1 scene 5 present Lady Macbeth's thoughts and feelings about Macbeth? Write about:

- what Lady Macbeth's thoughts and feelings are about Macbeth at this early point in the play
- how Shakespeare shows these thoughts and feelings by the way he writes.

Higher

Part (a) How does the following extract from Act 1 scene 5 present Lady Macbeth's thoughts and feelings about Macbeth?

> LADY MACBETH   Glamis thou art, and Cawdor; and shalt be
> What thou art promised: yet do I fear thy nature;
> It is too full o' th' milk of human kindness
> To catch the nearest way. Thou wouldst be great;
> Art not without ambition, but without
> The illness should attend it: what thou wouldst highly,
> That wouldst thou holily; wouldst not play false,
> And yet wouldst wrongly win: thou'dst have, great Glamis,
> That which cries 'Thus thou must do', if thou have it;
> And that which rather thou dost fear to do
> Than wishest should be undone. Hie thee hither,
> That I may pour my spirits in thine ear,
> And chastise with the valour of my tongue
> All that impedes thee from the golden round,
> Which fate and metaphysical aid doth seem
> To have thee crown'd withal.

Foundation and Higher

Part (b) How are Lady Macbeth's feelings about Macbeth presented at another point in the play?

(30 marks)

Much Ado about Nothing

Foundation

Part (a) How does the following extract from Act 1 scene 1 present Benedick's thoughts about love and women? Write about:

- what Benedick thinks of love and women at this early point in the play
- how Shakespeare shows what Benedick thinks by the way he writes.

Higher

Part (a) How does the following extract from Act 1 scene 1 present Benedick's thoughts about love and women?

BENEDICK	Why, i' faith, methinks she's too low for a high praise, too brown for a fair praise and too little for a great praise: only this commendation I can afford her, that were she other than she is, she were unhandsome; and being no other but as she is, I do not like her.
CLAUDIO	Thou thinkest I am in sport: I pray thee tell me truly how thou likest her.
BENEDICK	Would you buy her, that you inquire after her?
CLAUDIO	Can the world buy such a jewel?
BENEDICK	Yea, and a case to put it into. But speak you this with a sad brow? or do you play the flouting Jack, to tell us Cupid is a good hare-finder and Vulcan a rare carpenter? Come, in what key shall a man take you, to go in the song?
CLAUDIO	In mine eye she is the sweetest lady that ever I looked on.
BENEDICK	I can see yet without spectacles and I see no such matter: there's her cousin, an she were not possessed with a fury, exceeds her as much in beauty as the first of May doth the last of December. But I hope you have no intent to turn husband, have you?
CLAUDIO	I would scarce trust myself, though I had sworn the contrary, if Hero would be my wife.
BENEDICK	Is't come to this? In faith, hath not the world one man but he will wear his cap with suspicion? Shall I never see a bachelor of three-score again? Go to, i' faith; an thou wilt needs thrust thy neck into a yoke, wear the print of it and sigh away Sundays.

Foundation and Higher

Part (b) How are Benedick's thoughts about love and women presented at another point in the play?

(30 marks)

Romeo and Juliet

Foundation

Part (a) How does Shakespeare present conflict in the following extract from Act 1 scene 5? Write about:

* who is getting into conflict and why
* how Shakespeare shows this by the way he writes.

Higher

Part (a) How does Shakespeare present conflict in the following extract from Act 1 scene 5?

TYBALT	Uncle, this is a Montague, our foe,
	A villain that is hither come in spite,
	To scorn at our solemnity this night.
CAPULET	Young Romeo is it?
TYBALT	'Tis he, that villain Romeo.
CAPULET	Content thee, gentle coz, let him alone;
	He bears him like a portly gentleman;
	And, to say truth, Verona brags of him
	To be a virtuous and well-govern'd youth:
	I would not for the wealth of all the town
	Here in my house do him disparagement:
	Therefore be patient, take no note of him:
	It is my will, the which if thou respect,
	Show a fair presence and put off these frowns,
	An ill-beseeming semblance for a feast.
TYBALT	It fits, when such a villain is a guest:
	I'll not endure him.
CAPULET	He shall be endured:
	What, goodman boy! I say, he shall: go to;
	Am I the master here, or you? Go to.
	You'll not endure him! God shall mend my soul!
	You'll make a mutiny among my guests!
	You will set cock-a-hoop, you'll be the man!
TYBALT	Why, uncle, 'tis a shame.
CAPULET	Go to, go to;
	You are a saucy boy: is't so, indeed?
	This trick may chance to scathe you, I know what:
	You must contrary me! Marry, 'tis time.
	Well said, my hearts! You are a princox; go:
	Be quiet, or--More light, more light! For shame!
	I'll make you quiet.

Foundation and Higher

Part (b)   How does Shakespeare present conflict in another part of the play?   *(30 marks)*

Twelfth Night

Foundation

Part (a)   How does Shakespeare create comedy in the following extract from Act 1 scene 5? Write about:
- which characters are funny and why
- how Shakespeare gets this across through the way he writes.

Higher

Part (a)   How does Shakespeare create comedy in the following extract from Act 1 scene 5?

Enter SIR TOBY BELCH	
OLIVIA	By mine honour, half drunk. What is he at the gate, cousin?
SIR TOBY BELCH	A gentleman.
OLIVIA	A gentleman! what gentleman?
SIR TOBY BELCH	'Tis a gentle man here – *[Belches]* a plague o' these pickle-herring! How now, sot!
CLOWN	Good Sir Toby!
OLIVIA	Cousin, cousin, how have you come so early by this lethargy?
SIR TOBY BELCH	Lechery? I defy lechery. There's one at the gate.
OLIVIA	Ay, marry, what is he?
SIR TOBY BELCH	Let him be the devil, and he will, I care not: give me faith, say I. Well, it's all one.
[Exit]	
OLIVIA	What's a drunken man like, fool?
CLOWN	Like a drowned man, a fool and a mad man: one draught above heat makes him a fool; the second mads him; and a third drowns him.
OLIVIA	Go thou and seek the crowner, and let him sit o' my coz; for he's in the third degree of drink, he's drowned: go, look after him.
CLOWN	He is but mad yet, madonna; and the fool shall look to the madman.

Foundation and Higher

Part (b)   How does Shakespeare create comedy in another scene from the play?   *(30 marks)*

Julius Caesar

Foundation

Part (a)   How does Shakespeare present the character of Brutus in the following extract from Act 2 scene 1? Write about:
- what Brutus is like and how he wants to appear in this scene
- how Shakespeare shows this by the way he writes.

Higher

Part (a)   How does Shakespeare present the character of Brutus in the following extract from Act 2 scene 1?

CASSIUS	Let Antony and Caesar fall together.
BRUTUS	Our course will seem too bloody, Caius Cassius,
	To cut the head off and then hack the limbs,
	Like wrath in death and envy afterwards;
	For Antony is but a limb of Caesar:
	Let us be sacrificers, but not butchers, Caius.
	We all stand up against the spirit of Caesar;

(Cont.)

> *(Cont.)*
>
> And in the spirit of men there is no blood:
> O, that we then could come by Caesar's spirit,
> And not dismember Caesar! But, alas,
> Caesar must bleed for it! And, gentle friends,
> Let's kill him boldly, but not wrathfully;
> Let's carve him as a dish fit for the gods,
> Not hew him as a carcass fit for hounds:
> And let our hearts, as subtle masters do,
> Stir up their servants to an act of rage,
> And after seem to chide 'em. This shall make
> Our purpose necessary and not envious:
> Which so appearing to the common eyes,
> We shall be call'd purgers, not murderers.
> And for Mark Antony, think not of him;
> For he can do no more than Caesar's arm
> When Caesar's head is off.

Foundation and Higher

Part (b) How does Shakespeare present Brutus in another part of the play?   *(30 marks)*

Unit 4 Section B

Pride and Prejudice

Foundation

Part (a) How do you respond to Mr Bennet in the novel, and how does Austen make you respond by the way she writes? Write about:
- what you think about what Mr Bennet says and does
- how Austen makes you feel as you do by the way she writes.

Part (b) How do Mr Bennet's attitudes and behaviour show some of the values of the society in which he lives?

Higher

What is the importance of Mr Bennet in the novel? How does Austen's presentation of Mr Bennet reflect the social context of the novel?   *(24 marks)*

Wuthering Heights

Foundation

Part (a) How do you respond to the way different classes behave or are treated in the novel, and how does Brontë make you respond by the way she writes? Write about:
- two characters that belong to different classes, and how they behave or are treated
- how Brontë makes you feel about these characters and their class.

Part (b)   How does the behaviour and treatment of different classes reflect the values of society at the time the novel is set?

Higher

How does Brontë present class in the novel? How does Brontë's presentation of class reflect the society in which the characters live?   *(24 marks)*

Great Expectations

Foundation

Part (a)   How do you respond to the character of Estella, and how does Dickens make you respond by the way he writes? Write about:
*   different things that Estella says or does
*   how Dickens makes you feel about these things by the way he writes.

Part (b)   How does the character of Estella reflect the society in which she lives?

Higher

How does Dickens present Estella at two different points in the novel? How is Estella's life affected by the society in which she lives?   *(24 marks)*

'The Withered Arm' and Other Wessex Tales

Foundation

Part (a)   How do you respond to the character of Mr Stockdale in *'The Distracted Preacher'*, and how does Hardy make you respond by the way he writes? Write about:
*   different things that Mr Stockdale says or does
*   how Hardy makes you feel about these things by the way he writes.

Part (b)   How does the character of Mr Stockdale show some of the values of the time in which he is living?

Higher

How does Hardy present Mr Stockdale in *'The Distracted Preacher'*, and how does he reflect the cultural context of the story?   *(24 marks)*

Animal Farm

Foundation

Part (a)   How does Orwell show the importance of hopes and dreams in the novel, and how is this conveyed by the way he writes? Write about:
*   the different hopes and dreams that characters have, and why they are important
*   how Orwell shows their importance by the way he writes.

Part (b)   How do the hopes and dreams that Orwell describes relate to how people think and behave in society?

Higher

How does Orwell use hopes and dreams in the novel, and how does this reflect ideas about society?

(24 marks)

Quality of Written Communication

The examiner will be considering the quality of your writing in all your exams, but **in Unit 1 there's also a specific allocation of four marks for your accuracy of written communication**. You must take care with your use of standard English, and **ensure that your handwriting is legible**.

Below are some tips about spelling, punctuation and grammar to help you avoid common mistakes.

Spelling

- Learn how to spell the title of the two texts you have studied in Unit 1, along with the surnames of the two authors.
- Learn simple key words. For example: play, poem, novel; imagery, simile, metaphor; verb, adjective, adverb; language, structure, form; character, speaker, narrator.
- Learn how to spell connective phrases. For example: in comparison, in contrast, however, whereas, similarly.

- Don't make spelling mistakes with words that have already been given to you by the examiner, such as those in the exam question.
- If you're copying down a quotation from the text, copy it accurately so you don't make careless spelling mistakes.

Punctuation

- Don't let your sentences get too long and remember full stop + capital letter. (If you use 'and' more than once in a sentence, it's getting too long.)
- Remember to put 'quotation marks' at the start and end of all your quotations.
- Introduce a quotation with a comma (,) or a colon (:). Don't use a dash (–) or a semi-colon (;).

- When you're listing things, separate each item or idea with a comma.
- As well as grouping your ideas into clear sentences, organise your sentences into clear paragraphs.

Grammar

- Remember to use capital letters for the names of people, places, and the titles of poems, novels and plays.
- Don't confuse 'have' with 'of'. For example, would've should be written 'would have' not 'would of'.
- Learn: there (place), their (ownership) and they're (abbreviation of they are).

- Learn: its (a pronoun like his / her) and it's (abbreviation of it is).
- Write about the *effect* of a piece of writing (noun), and how a piece of writing *affects* the reader (verb).

Spelling, Punctuation and Grammar

Read these examples of students' answers to the Unit 1 exam and try to correct them. Check your answers on page 85.

1. For the first example, focus on correcting thirteen spelling errors:

> ... Our fist impresion of Mrs Rutter is given to us through Pat's words to Sandra. The two ajectives make Mrs Rutter seem sweet and harmless. This is emphised by the use of the nown 'thing', as if Mrs Rutter is almost forgetable, and the sugestion that she needs looking after or protecting. The auther increases this image of vulnrability when Pat tells us that Mrs Ruter recieves 'home help' and has a 'wonky leg after her op'. The slang word 'wonky' sounds quite funny, as if Mrs Rutter might be a quite comical caracter in the storey.

2. In the next example, try to find the nine mistakes linked to punctuation:

> Susan Hill creates suspense in her opening chapter when Arthur tell's the reader, Yes, I had a story, a true story, a story of haunting and evil, fear and confusion, horror and tragedy. The three pair's create a sinister atmosphere by warning what the rest of the novel will contain with the final pair suggesting death. this is increased by Arthurs insistence that this is a 'true story' and he also shows discomfort in the idea of telling his story, which is conveyed through the pauses created by the short clauses Hill adds to the suspense by using a metaphor to tell us how strongly the experience has affected Arthur 'it was now woven into my very fibres'.

3. For the third example, check the student's use of grammar and look for nine errors.

> Steinbeck shows george's power over lennie through the way that he speaks to him, 'You know God damn well what. I want that mouse. [...] Blubberin' like a baby! Jesus Christ!' The short sentences and exclamation marks suggest the forceful tone with which he addresses Lennie. He adds to this affect by his use of profanity, as well as the simile (and it's childish verb) that he uses to insulted and demean Lennie. We can also see his power in the way that his first sentence informs Lennie that he ain't fooled, and the second sentence is a firm order. Steinbeck adds too this by havin George use a rhetorical question to threatened Lennie with violence, 'do I have to sock you?'.

4. Finally, correct this example for spelling, punctuation and grammar. There are twenty-one mistakes to find:

> Mr watts is present as a very unusual figure 'Pop Eye was the only white for miles around, little kids stared at him until their ice blocks melted over their black hands. Older kids sucked in their breath and knocked on his door to ask to do their 'school project' on him. The use of the nickname pop eye sugests a lack of respect for Mr Watts, but it comes more from his status as an outsider This is shown by the image of the children starring for a long amount of time the contarst of 'black' and 'white', and the addjective 'only'. The fact that student's wanting too do their projects on him also suggest he is seen as unusuall or mysterious the description of the students breathing deeply suggests Mr Watts was also a figure of fear, agaiin dew to him being an outsider rather than him bein a bad person.

The following notes are not specific to the text you've studied but should give you a guide to the points you should be thinking about.

Page 5

1. Look at how characters are described and what others say about them.

2. Think about the character's behaviour, descriptions or stage directions that we're given, and how they speak to people.

3. Look at how the character behaves around others, how they speak to people, and how others speak to them.

4. Consider which character does the most, speaks the most or has the biggest effect on the story.

Page 7

1. Look at how the character alters the way they behave or speak, and how they think or behave towards other characters who change.

2. Think about how their different behaviour affects characters and events in the story in a positive or negative way.

3. Look at specific events, whether personal to a character or on a broader scale, and why they affect people.

4. Consider which characters get on better or worse, or whether any characters swap roles.

Page 9

1. Explore how the setting is conveyed through descriptions or stage directions and what people say.

2. Think about how the setting links to different characters and their behaviour, and whether the characters fit into their setting or seem outsiders.

3. Consider how the events of the story are affected by the time and place in which the story is set.

4. Look at ways in which the setting creates or reflects different feelings, such as happiness, relaxation, fear or sadness.

Page 11

1. Decide what the biggest idea is in the book, and how this is shown through events and characters.

2. Look at how what happens in the story helps to convey one of the author's main ideas.

3. Consider how the author uses characters to convey their main ideas.

4. Think about the main ideas in the story and which characters might be on opposite sides of a discussion about each idea.

Page 15

1. Think about which scenes contain events, description or dialogue that tell us about, or link to, the time and place in which the story is set.

2. Look at how the thoughts, speech and behaviour of characters is different to what you'd expect from people today.

3. Think about which events are caused, wholly or partly, by what society is like in the story.

4. Consider whether the time and place in which the story is set creates more sympathy, disapproval or perhaps shock towards the characters and events.

Page 17

1. Consider how characters speak and behave and how this affects your response to them.

2. Think about how sympathy is created for a character through their actions, the things that happen to them and how other characters treat them.

3. Explore how the characters behave, how they speak to people, and how they affect the events and other characters of the story.

4. Look at the characters in the novel who don't appear a great deal, but have a big effect on the story through what they do, say or represent.

Page 19

1. Explore how the character alters the way they behave or speak, and how they react to changes in other characters.

2. Look at how their different behaviour affects characters and events in the story in a positive or negative way.

3. Consider specific events, whether personal to a character or on a broader scale, and why they affect people.

4. Think about which characters get on better or worse, or whether any characters swap roles.

Page 21

1. Decide what the biggest idea is in the book and how this is shown through events and characters.

2. Think about how what happens in the story helps to convey one of the author's main ideas.

3. Look at how the author uses characters to convey their main ideas.

4. Consider the main ideas in the story and which characters might be on opposite sides of a discussion about each idea.

Page 33

1. Make sure that the two poems have clear similarities and differences that you could explore.

2. You could look at *The Clown Punk*, *Horse Whisperer*, *Medusa*, *Singh Song!*, *Les Grands Seigneurs*, and *The Hunchback in the Park*.

3. Consider which poems you remember the most clearly or which ones surprised you most when you first read them.

4. Explore how the poet's choice of images shows changes in *Horse Whisperer*, *Medusa* and *Les Grands Seigneurs*. You could also look at how *The Ruined Maid* and *On a Portrait of a Deaf Man* show the past and present of a character.

Quick Tests: Notes and Guidance

Page 35

1. Make sure that the two poems have clear similarities and differences that you could explore.
2. You could look at *A Vision, The Moment, Price We Pay for the Sun, Neighbours, The Prelude, Below the Green Corrie, Storm in the Black Forest,* and *Wind.*
3. Think about which poems you remember the most clearly or which ones impressed you most when you first read them.
4. Consider how positive images appear in *The Vision, Crossing the Loch* and *The Wild Swans at Coole,* whilst negative images appear in *Price We Pay for the Sun, Neighbours, London, Spellbound,* and *Wind.*

Page 37

1. Make sure that the two poems have clear similarities and differences that you could explore.
2. You could look at *Mametz Wood, Belfast Confetti, Poppies, Bayonet Charge,* and *The Falling Leaves.*
3. Think about which poems you remember the most clearly or which ones struck you most when you first read them.
4. Look at how emotions are conveyed in *Out of the Blue, Mametz Wood, Belfast Confetti, Poppies, Futility, The Charge of the Light Brigade,* and *Bayonet Charge.*

Page 39

1. Make sure that the two poems have clear similarities and differences that you could explore.
2. You could look at *The Manhunt, Hour, Quickdraw, Ghazal, Praise Song for My Mother, To His Coy Mistress,* and *The Farmer's Bride.*
3. Consider which poems you remember the most clearly or which ones surprised you most when you first read them.
4. Think about which poems convey romantic love, family love, regret, or hope in a powerful way.

Page 43

1. You may have considered how he seems normal but dissatisfied, how he is aggressive and proud of his violence and how he is disturbing.
2. At first he doesn't seem to have any reason for the murder. However, the speaker contrasts what he sees as his lack of freedom with the hitchhiker's independence, which suggests jealousy. He also points out a similarity with the hitchhiker, which could be suggesting self-hatred.
3. Look at how the sense of everyday normality continues and how the speaker makes a joke about what he has done. Consider how this affects the atmosphere of the poem and what you feel about the speaker.
4. Think about how the dramatic monologue allows Simon Armitage to explore the mind of a murderer in a sinister and unusual way.

Page 45

1. You may have considered how death is described quite nicely at first, but then her descriptions become more negative with a stronger sense of finality.
2. Look at which images or ideas might make the poem moving. Alternatively, think about how it could seem consoling or depressing.
3. Think about what you feel the last lines mean, and how these are meant to affect the person the poem is addressed to. Compare these lines with the title, and consider why there is a contrast.
4. Think about the effect that the poem is meant to have on the person the poet is addressing and what thoughts and feelings the poet must have had at the time she was writing.

Page 53

1. Consider what words could sum up how each character behaves and feels.
2. Think about the things the character does, how they speak to people and how others speak to them.
3. Look at how the character behaves around others, how they speak to people and how others speak to them.
4. Explore which character does the most, speaks the most, or has the biggest effect on the play.

Page 55

1. Look at how the character alters the way they behave or speak, and how they react to other characters who change.
2. Think about how their different behaviour affects characters and events in the play.
3. Explore specific events and why they affect people.

Page 57

1. Look at how the thoughts, speech and behaviour of characters is different to what you'd expect from people today.
2. Think about which events are caused, wholly or partly, by what society is like in the play.
3. Explore scenes that contain events or speech that tell us about, or link to, the time and place in which the play is set.

Page 59

1. Consider what the biggest theme is in the play, and how this is shown through events and characters.
2. Look at how what happens in the story helps to convey one of Shakespeare's main themes.
3. Explore how Shakespeare uses characters to convey his main themes, either through the things they do or the things they say.
4. Think about scenes that contain events or speech that present or develop one of Shakespeare's themes.

Page 61

1. Look back at the language techniques and decide which one you think has most helped to convey the characters or themes of the play.

2. Think about the stagecraft and consider where it has been used most successfully to convey the characters or themes of the play.

3. Look at the language techniques that Shakespeare puts into the character's speech in order to tell us about them. Consider how this is developed by how these lines are then performed on stage.

Page 65

1. Decide which character has had the most impact on you, because of how they are described, how they behave and the things they say.

2. Think about how sympathy is created for a character because of what happens to them, how other's talk about them and how they are described.

3. Explore how a character's behaviour and speech, combined with the way they are described, makes you like or dislike them.

Page 67

1. Look at how the character alters the way they behave or speak, and how the author describes them differently.

2. Consider how their different behaviour affects other characters, events and their own lives.

3. Think about specific events (whether personal to a character or on a broader scale), as well as the novel's context, and why these things affect the characters.

Page 69

1. Think about how the thoughts, speech and behaviour of characters is affected by where and when the novel is set.

2. Consider which events are caused, wholly or partly, by what society is like in the novel.

Page 71

1. Decide what the biggest idea is in the novel, and how this is shown through events and characters.

2. Look at how what happens in the story helps to convey one of the author's main ideas.

3. Consider how the author uses characters to convey a theme, through their behaviour, their speech or how they are described.

Page 73

1. Look back at the notes about the author's style and find typical examples of description, characterisation or speech.

2. Think about how the style of writing affects how much you like, dislike, feel sympathetic towards, or are surprised by, a character.

3. Consider how the writer's style makes different events more interesting, moving, shocking or pleasing.

Spelling, Punctuation and Grammar Examples

Page 82

1. ... Our first impression of Mrs Rutter is given to us through Pat's words to Sandra. The two adjectives make Mrs Rutter seem sweet and harmless. This is emphasised by the use of the noun 'thing', as if Mrs Rutter is almost forgettable, and the suggestion that she needs looking after or protecting. The author increases this image of vulnerability when Pat tells us that Mrs Rutter receives 'home help' and has a 'wonky leg after her op'. The slang word 'wonky' sounds quite funny, as if Mrs Rutter might be a quite comical character in the story.

2. Susan Hill creates suspense in her opening chapter when Arthur tells the reader, 'Yes, I had a story, a true story, a story of haunting and evil, fear and confusion, horror and tragedy'. The three pairs create a sinister atmosphere by warning what the rest of the novel will contain, with the final pair suggesting death. This is increased by Arthur's insistence that this is a 'true story' and he also shows discomfort in the idea of telling his story, which is conveyed through the pauses created by the short clauses. Hill adds to the suspense by using a metaphor to tell us how strongly the experience has affected Arthur, 'it was now woven into my very fibres'.

3. Steinbeck shows George's power over Lennie through the way that he speaks to him, 'You know God damn well what. I want that mouse. [...] Blubberin' like a baby! Jesus Christ!' The short sentences and exclamation marks suggest the forceful tone with which he addresses Lennie. He adds to this effect by his use of profanity, as well as the simile (and its childish verb) that he uses to insult and demean Lennie. We can also see his power in the way that his first sentence informs Lennie that he isn't fooled, and the second sentence is a firm order. Steinbeck adds to this by having George use a rhetorical question to threaten Lennie with violence, 'do I have to sock you?'.

4. Mr Watts is presented as a very unusual figure, 'Pop Eye was the only white for miles around, little kids stared at him until their ice blocks melted over their black hands. Older kids sucked in their breath and knocked on his door to ask to do their 'school project' on him'. The use of the nickname Pop Eye suggests a lack of respect for Mr Watts, but it comes more from his status as an outsider. This is shown by the image of the children staring for a long amount of time, the contrast of 'black' and 'white', and the adjective 'only'. The fact that students want to do their projects on him also suggests he is seen as unusual or mysterious. The description of the students breathing deeply suggests Mr Watts was also a figure of fear, again due to him being an outsider rather than him being a bad person.

Answers to Exam Practice Questions

Look at the mark scheme from D to A*, noticing how the skills that the examiner wants to see you using gradually build up.

Remember that if you are entered for Foundation Tier you will not be able to achieve a grade higher than C.

D	• Come up with a range of comments. • Show awareness of the idea or theme specified in the question. • Support comments with some quotations. • Identify some effects of language, structure or form.
C	• Sustained, focused comments. • Clear focus on the idea or theme specified in the question. • All comments supported by relevant quotations. • Explanation of how language and structure convey meaning and/or affect the reader.
B	• Thorough interpretation. • Thoughtful, well-organised response to the question. • Well-chosen quotations that allow some detailed analysis related to the question. • Appreciation of some of the range of effects created by language, structure and form.
A	• Thorough exploration and interpretation. • Mature, well-organised response to the question. • Precisely chosen quotations that allow a range of detailed analysis related to the question. • Analysis of a range of effects created by language, structure and form.
A*	• Insightful exploration and interpretation. • Mature, convincing and imaginative response to the question. • Precisely chosen quotations that allow a range of close, detailed analysis related to the question. • Analysis and evaluation of the full range of effects created by language, structure and form.

Getting From D to C

Notice that the main differences between a D and a C are making sure that all your comments are focused on the question (not just some), ensuring that all your points are supported by quotations (not just some), and trying to explain *how* language and structure help to convey meaning (rather than just saying *what* the writer has written).

Getting From B to A/A*

Notice that the main differences between a B and an A / A* are exploring the text and showing insight into how it works (so if you've made a good point, try to develop it before you move on to your next idea), and offering a full range of analysis (interpreting lots of different techniques of language, structure and form, rather than always simply analysing imagery). The A* also asks for evaluative comments, whereby you try to weigh up which techniques are more successful than others in achieving the writer's aims.

Spelling, Punctuation and Grammar

There will also be up to four marks awarded for the accuracy of your writing in Unit 1. You will be awarded one of four levels:

Level 1	Spelling, punctuation and grammar used with some accuracy. Errors may obstruct meaning and specialist terms are used incorrectly.
Level 2	Spelling, punctuation and grammar used with reasonable accuracy. Errors do not obstruct meaning and some specialist terms are used correctly.
Level 3	Spelling, punctuation and grammar used with considerable accuracy. A good range of specialist terms are used correctly.
Level 4	Spelling, punctuation and grammar used with consistent accuracy. A wide range of specialist terms are used correctly.

You must take care with your use of Standard English. Don't forget: clear handwriting, correct spelling, accurate use of capital letters and punctuation, effective use of quotation marks, and paragraphs to separate your ideas.

Unit 1 Section A: Content

The bullet points below are to help you understand the sort of content that the examiner would be looking for in your exam answer. The examiner would then use the mark scheme to work out how skilled you have been in your exploration and analysis of the text.

Sunlight on the Grass – Anthology

Foundation

Part (a)

- Exploration of how Mrs Rutter is initially presented as old, kind and sweet.
- Exploration of how the author develops her character, making her increasingly sinister, callous and oblivious to the boy's reaction.
- Consideration of how Mrs Rutter's character is formed by her experiences of war.

Part (b)

- Exploration of how the character comes across through descriptions, speech and the views of others.
- Exploration of how the character develops during the story.

Higher

Part (a)

- Exploration of how Carla feels like an outsider, but how writing to Steve gives her life more meaning or pleasure.
- Exploration of her fear of how meeting Steve would ruin their relationship.
- Exploration of her delight in actually meeting Steve.

Part (b)

- Exploration of how feelings come across through descriptions and speech.
- Exploration of how feelings change during the story.

Lord of the Flies

Foundation

- Exploration of how Jack treats people, such as the choir and Piggy.
- Exploration of how he reacts when Ralph is made leader.
- Exploration of Jack's positive and negative qualities, especially in terms of leadership.
- Exploration of comments made about Jack, for instance by Sam and Eric.

Higher

- Exploration of the different leadership qualities shown by Jack and Ralph.
- Exploration of the difficulties of leadership as shown by Ralph.
- Exploration of how the power that comes with leadership can corrupt.

- Exploration of why Piggy could make a good leader but would never become one.

Martyn Pig

Foundation

- Exploration of how Alex comes across in a positive, sympathetic way.
- Exploration of how this characterisation is affected by Martyn's unreliable narrative.
- Exploration of how the writer gradually shows us the negative side of Alex.
- Exploration of how the reader responds to her final actions in the novel.

Higher

- Exploration of how Martyn is treated by his dad and what he feels about this.
- Exploration of how Martyn treats his father and how he feels after he has killed him.
- Exploration of how Martyn is treated by Jean, what he feels about this, and how he treats her.

Touching the Void

Foundation

- Exploration of how Simon Yates comes across at the start of the novel from things he says and does.
- Exploration of how Simon tries to help Joe.
- Exploration of how the reader responds to the decision Simon has to make about cutting the rope.
- Exploration of Simon's thoughts and behaviour after he has cut the rope.

Higher

- Exploration of how the opening creates tension by preparing us for what is going to happen.
- Exploration of how tension and excitement is created through the odds gradually stacking up against the two men.
- Exploration of how tension is created around the decision to cut the rope.
- Exploration of how excitement is created as we discover the way the men survive.

The Woman in Black

Foundation

- Exploration of the graveyard and the house's isolation.
- Exploration of the creepy appearance of the house.
- Exploration of the use of darkness and noise inside.
- Exploration of how the nursery is made sinister.

Answers to Exam Practice Questions

Higher
- Exploration of how chapter 1 introduces us to Arthur's fears, the idea of ghosts, and the sense that a terrible experience has blighted his life.
- Exploration of how chapters 2 and 3 build up a sense that Arthur is underestimating what he is getting into.
- Exploration of how chapters 2 and 3 build up mystery about Eel Marsh House and Mrs Drablow.

Under Milk Wood

Foundation
- Exploration of how Llareggub is linked to beauty and mystery.
- Exploration of how the village is made to seem busy by the varied people we meet.
- Exploration of how the village is full of secrecy and discontent.
- Exploration of how Llareggub is sometimes presented as a comic place.

Higher
- Exploration of the passionate love between Mr Edwards and Myfanwy, and how it is restricted to letters and dreams.
- Exploration of the forbidden love of Gossamer and Sinbad Sailors.
- Exploration of the devotion shown by Mrs Owens.
- Exploration of the fantasy love of Lily Smalls and Mae Rose Cottage.

The Crucible

Foundation
- Exploration of how Hale is presented in Act 1, and the audience's response to this.
- Exploration of how Hale's questioning of John and Elizabeth, plus his misjudgement of the trials, alters our view of him.
- Exploration of how Hale's gradual disillusionment and eventual criticism of the trials affects our view of him.
- Exploration of how we respond to Hale's final words.

Higher
- Exploration of how the opening of Act 2 shows the flaws in their relationship.
- Exploration of how the end of Act 2 and Act 3 show the strengths in their relationship.
- Exploration of how Act 4 shows John and Elizabeth finally being honest with each other about their own faults in order to heal their relationship.
- Exploration of their final words to, and about, each other.

Kindertransport

Foundation
- Exploration of how the historical context of the play is used in the text.
- Exploration of how different points in the play are made moving. For example: Helga sending Eva away, Eva/Evelyn's visions of the Ratcatcher, Eva's decision not to go with Helga later in the play, Faith's relationship with her mother.

Higher
- Exploration of Eva/Evelyn's struggle with her identity (being sent away, creating a new life, rejecting her old life when it returns, and keeping things secret).
- Exploration of Faith's need to understand her mother and her mother's past.

An Inspector Calls

Foundation
- Exploration of how the Inspector points blame at different characters.
- Exploration of Arthur's role in Eva's death.
- Exploration of how Eric and Gerald exploit Eva as a woman, and how Sybil and Shiela mistreat her due to her class.
- Exploration of how the above things represent the social forces that lead to her suicide.

Higher
- Exploration of the play's structure, and how information is gradually revealed to us (and to the characters on stage).
- Exploration of how different characters react to the things that are revealed.
- Exploration of how conflict is created in the play.

Deoxyribonucleic Acid (DNA)

Foundation
- Exploration of the behaviour/events leading up to the incident with Adam.
- Exploration of how different characters feel or behave in the play, due to the pressures of the gang. For example: how Danny comes across as an outsider; John Tate's role as leader; Richard's behaviour towards John; Brian being expected to 'identify' the innocent man; how people behave around Phil.

Higher
- Exploration of how Lea and Phil are presented when we first meet them.
- Exploration of different ways in which we see the power that Phil has over Lea.
- Exploration of how we are shown the relationship changing, with Lea gaining more power and then leaving.

Unit 1 Section B: Content

The bullet points below are to help you understand the sort of content that the examiner would be looking for in your exam answer. The examiner would then use the mark scheme to work out how skilled you have been in your exploration and analysis of the text.

Of Mice and Men

Foundation and Higher

Part (a)

- Exploration of George's speech: orders, threats, swearing, short sentences, exclamation, simile, rhetorical question.
- Exploration of descriptions of how George treats Lennie: verbs, adverbs.
- Exploration of how Lennie behaves in front of George: verbs, adverbs, adjectives, simile.

Part (b)

- Exploration of power through another character, with links made to historical context. For example: Curley (physical power, plus economic power as the boss's son); Curley's wife (economic power as the boss's daughter-in-law; racial power over Crooks); Crooks (intelligence over Lennie; but less social power due to colour).

Purple Hibiscus

Foundation and Higher

Part (a)

- Exploration of Mama's kindness, reason, gratitude, plainness, traditional views of women, vulnerability, love of her sister-in-law.
- Exploration of description and speech: verbs, adjectives, rhetorical question, ellipsis.

Part (b)

- Exploration of how father dominates and mistreats wife and daughter, and how this is portrayed as socially accepted (including by Mama). Possible link to the Church's role in this.
- Exploration of how Ifeoma is presented as something unusual, but is also struggling financially, is unfairly dismissed, and leaves for America.

Mister Pip

Foundation and Higher

Part (a)

- Exploration of how Mr Watts is treated as something unusual; his difference is frightening and his colour links him to traditional ideas of superiority that are now passing; he is also mocked for his appearance.

- Exploration of his intelligence, which he shows off, as well as his mystery and kindness.
- Exploration of description and speech: verbs, adverbs, adjectives, list form, short sentence.

Part (b)

- Exploration of different attitudes towards white people, linked to the cultural context. For example, curiosity, distrust, traditional respect and colonial bitterness.

To Kill a Mockingbird

Foundation and Higher

Part (a)

- Exploration of how every town has a family like the Ewells: use of adjectives, list form and contrast.
- Exploration of the Ewell family house: use of adjectives, verbs, adverbs, simile, list form, metaphor and humorous aside by narrator. Sense of enclosure and toughness, as well as hardship and dirt.

Part (b)

- Exploration of Bob Ewell, linked to social/historical context.
- Exploration of Bob's drunkenness, violence, the events linked to the accusation about Tom, his behaviour in court, and his vengeful behaviour after the trial.
- Exploration of others' reactions to Bob, such as Scout's criticism and the narrator's sarcasm.

Follow the Rabbit-Proof Fence

Foundation and Higher

Part (a)

- Exploration of Martu norms (contrasted with the norms of the whites): use of verbs, adverbs and adjectives.
- Exploration of their sense of humour, curiosity and politeness/selflessness linked to the clothes: use of metaphor and verbs.
- Exploration of their beliefs/rituals (protection from spirits, mourning) and ways of life (hunting).

Part (b)

- Exploration of the different groups during history, for example the contrasting beliefs, behaviour and values of the colonialists and the natives.
- Exploration of how different groups, white and black, respond to people of mixed race.

Answers to Exam Practice Questions

Look at the mark scheme from D to A*, noticing how the skills that the examiner wants to see you using gradually build up.

Remember that if you are entered for Foundation Tier you will not be able to achieve a grade higher than C.

D	• Come up with a range of comments.
	• Show awareness of the idea or theme specified in the question.
	• Support comments with some quotations.
	• Identify some effects of language, structure or form.
	• Structured comments on similarities and differences in ideas, meaning and techniques.
C	• Sustained, focused comments.
	• Clear focus on the idea or theme specified in the question.
	• All comments supported by relevant quotations.
	• Explanation of how language and structure convey meaning and/or affect the reader.
	• Sustained focus on similarities and differences in ideas, meaning and techniques.
B	• Thorough interpretation.
	• Thoughtful, well-organised response to the question.
	• Well-chosen quotations that allow some detailed analysis related to the question.
	• Appreciation of some of the range of effects created by language, structure and form.
	• Developed comparison of ideas, meaning and techniques.
A	• Thorough exploration and interpretation.
	• Mature, well-organised response to the question.
	• Precisely chosen quotations that allow a range of detailed analysis related to the question.
	• Analysis of a range of effects created by language, structure and form.
	• Analytical comparison of ideas, meaning and techniques.
A*	• Insightful exploration and interpretation.
	• Mature, convincing and imaginative response to the question.
	• Precisely chosen quotations that allow a range of close, detailed analysis related to the question.
	• Analysis and evaluation of the full range of effects created by language, structure and form.
	• Evaluative comparison of ideas, meanings and techniques.

Getting From D to C

Notice that the main differences between a D and a C are making sure that all your comments are focused on the question (not just some), ensuring that all your points are supported by quotations (not just some), and trying to explain how language and structure help to convey meaning (rather than just saying what the writers have written). Comparison must be kept up throughout the essay.

Getting From B to A/A*

Notice that the main differences between a B and an A/A* are exploring the text and showing insight into how it works (so if you've made a good point, trying to develop it before you move on to your next idea), and offering a full range of analysis and comparison (interpreting lots of different techniques of language, structure and form, rather than always simply analysing imagery). The A* also asks for evaluative comments and comparison, whereby you try to weigh up which techniques are more successful than others in achieving the writer's aims.

Unit 2 Section A: Content

The bullet points below are to help you understand the sort of content that the examiner would be looking for in your exam answer. The examiner would then use the mark scheme to work out how skilled you have been in your comparison and analysis of the poems. Remember that the examiner will be expecting you to compare the poems.

Character and Voice

Foundation

- Exploration of how the speaker in *Medusa* is presented as aggressive, obsessive, frightening and disgusted with herself.
- Exploration of use of lists, metaphor, simile, sibilance, rhetorical question, repetition, verbs, short sentences; irregular form to perhaps suggest a lack of self-control.
- Comparison with, for example: *Horse Whisperer, Les Grands Seigneurs, Give, My Last Duchess,* or *The River God.*

Higher

- Exploration of how women are presented in *The Ruined Maid* as impressed by riches, reliant on or exploited by men, having a difficult life with few choices if they come from a lower class.
- Exploration of use of exclamation, verbs, adjectives, dialect vs standard or formal English, simile, repetition, short sentence; duologue; controlled use of rhyming couplets and quatrains perhaps reflects the lack of freedom the two women have (regardless of the different path they took in life).
- Comparison with, for example: *Medusa, Singh Song!, Les Grands Seigneurs,* or *My Last Duchess.*

Place

Foundation

- Exploration of how the poet feels *London* is no longer free, but full of oppression, misery, child labour, an uncaring Church and monarchy, and sexual corruption that is destroying the innocence of the young.
- Exploration of use of repetition, adjectives, metaphor, anaphora, wordplay/double meaning, verbs; controlled use of rhythm and quatrains perhaps reflects the social restrictions that the poet is exploring.
- Comparison with, for example, one of the following: *A Vision, Price We Pay for the Sun, Neighbours, The Prelude,* or *Below the Green Corrie.*

Higher

- Exploration of how *Hard Water* presents ideas about identity, home, dialect, belonging and not belonging, and having mixed feelings about one's roots.
- Exploration of the use of adjectives, verbs, colloquialism, dialect, metaphor, short sentences, simile, repetition; the use of free verse could be to suggest the no-nonsense setting or reflect the flow of water.

- Comparison with, for example: *A Vision, The Moment, Price We Pay for the Sun, London,* or *Wind.*

Conflict

Foundation

- Exploration of how *Belfast Confetti* conveys the shock, sound, appearance and confusion of a riot or nail bomb attack, and how the poet reflects upon it.
- Exploration of the use of adverbs, metaphor, lists, verbs, adjectives, dash and ellipsis, rhetorical question, short sentence, pattern of three; use of free verse, with every other line carrying only a few words, to convey the sense of chaos and the speaker rushing in different directions to escape.
- Comparison with, for example: *The Charge of the Light Brigade,* or *Bayonet Charge.*

Higher

- Exploration of how *The Right Word* presents ideas about fear, suspicion, morality, beliefs, humanity, and who is 'right' during times of conflict.
- Exploration of the use of repetition, rhetorical question, verbs, pronouns, short sentence, simile, adverbs; use of short lines, and question and answer, to reflect the speaker's developing thoughts.
- Comparison with: *Mametz Wood, The Yellow Palm, At the Border 1979, Futility,* or *Come On, Come Back.*

Relationships

Foundation

- Exploration of how *Sonnet 43* conveys romantic love as immeasurable, complex yet simple, strong (almost worshipful), healing, and endless.
- Exploration of the use of question and answer, exclamation, anaphora, pattern of three, adverbs, metaphor; use of a sonnet (a traditional form of love poetry) to intensify emotion.
- Comparison with, for example: *The Manhunt, Hour, Quickdraw, Ghazal,* or *Sonnet 116.*

Higher

- Exploration of how *Brothers* presents family relationships through the speaker's feelings of irritation towards his younger brother when he was a boy; he reflects on his unkind actions with guilt, realising that it has affected their relationship ever since.
- Exploration of the use of verbs, adjectives, adverbs, metaphor, repetition, pronouns; use of aspects of a sonnet (a traditional form of love poetry) perhaps suggests his true feelings for his brother, despite his past actions, whilst the closed form emphasises that he cannot take back and change the past.
- Comparison with, for example: *Praise Song for My Mother, Harmonium, Sister Maude,* or *Nettles.*

Answers to Exam Practice Questions

The bullet points below are to help you understand the sort of content that the examiner would be looking for in your exam answer. The examiner would then use the mark scheme to work out how skilled you have been in your exploration and analysis of the poem.

Sample Question 1

- Exploration of how water is presented as scarce. Use of simile, short sentence, nouns, verbs, adjectives, alliteration, metaphor.
- Exploration of how water is valuable. Use of verbs, metaphor, pattern of three (without commas to suggest crowding together), lists, religious language, adjectives, nouns, personification.
- Exploration of form: short sentences and short, end-stopped stanzas at the beginning could suggest hopelessness or mirror the lack of water; change to longer sentences, more varied line lengths, and enjambment between stanzas could mirror the suddenness of the water escaping from the burst pipe, and people's excitement and delight.

Sample Question 2

- Exploration of how the poet conveys his love of summertime through descriptions of the weather, flowers and trees, rivers and lakes, animals and insects.
- Exploration of the use of verbs, alliteration (to link words together and suggest harmony), adjectives, metaphor, simile, personification, repetition.
- Exploration of form: sonnet (traditional form of love poetry) to emphasise his feelings; rhyming couplets link images together to suggest harmony in nature; lack of punctuation (even at the end of the poem) could suggest the immediacy of these feelings, and that the joys of summer are endless.

Unit 4 Sections A and B: Skills

Look at the mark scheme from D to A*, noticing how the skills that the examiner wants to see you using gradually build up.

Remember that if you are entered for Foundation Tier you will not be able to achieve a grade higher than C.

D	• Come up with a range of comments. • Show awareness of the idea or theme specified in the question. • Support comments with some quotations. • Identify some effects of language, structure or form.
C	• Sustained, focused comments. • Clear focus on the idea or theme specified in the question. • All comments supported by relevant quotations. • Explanation of how language and structure convey meaning and/or affect the reader.
B	• Thorough interpretation. • Thoughtful, well-organised response to the question. • Well-chosen quotations that allow some detailed analysis related to the question. • Appreciation of some of the range of effects created by language, structure and form.
A	• Thorough exploration and interpretation. • Mature, well-organised response to the question. • Precisely chosen quotations that allow a range of detailed analysis related to the question. • Analysis of a range of effects created by language, structure and form.

A*	• Insightful exploration and interpretation. • Mature, convincing and imaginative response to the question. • Precisely chosen quotations that allow a range of close, detailed analysis related to the question. • Analysis and evaluation of the full range of effects created by language, structure and form.

Getting From D to C

Notice that the main differences between a D and a C are making sure that all your comments are focused on the question (not just some), ensuring that all your points are supported by quotations (not just some), and trying to explain how language and structure help to convey meaning (rather than just saying what the writer has written).

Getting From B to A / A*

Notice that the main differences between a B and an A / A* are exploring the text and showing insight into how it works (so if you've made a good point, trying to develop it before you move on to your next idea), and offering a full range of analysis (interpreting lots of different techniques of language, structure and form, rather than always simply analysing imagery). The A* also asks for evaluative comments, whereby you try to weigh up which techniques are more successful than others in achieving the writer's aims.

Unit 4 Section A: Content

The bullet points below are to help you understand the sort of content that the examiner would be looking for in your exam answer. The examiner would then use the mark scheme to work out how skilled you have been in your exploration and analysis of the play.

Macbeth

Foundation and Higher
Part (a)

- Exploration of her belief in Macbeth's prospects and ambition, but thinks he is too nice to really achieve what he could. Use of repetition, metaphor, adjectives, verbs, adverbs, contrast.
- Exploration of how she believes she can influence him and banish his fears. Use of imperative, adjectives, verbs, metaphor.

Part (b)

- Exploration of another point in the play where we see Lady Macbeth's feelings about Macbeth. For example: when Macbeth decides against the murder but she convinces him; after the murder; the scene with Banquo's ghost.

Much Ado about Nothing

Foundation and Higher
Part (a)

- Exploration of Benedick's humorous criticism of Hero, contrasted with Claudio's romantic words. Use of adverbs, adjectives, repetition, contrast, rhetorical question.
- Exploration of Benedick's attitude towards women in general, for example only valuing them for their beauty. Use of adjectives, simile.
- Exploration of Benedick's attitude towards marriage, for example that it takes away a man's freedom. Use of rhetorical question, verb phrases, metaphor, short sentence.

Part (b)

- Exploration of another point in the play where we see Benedick's thoughts about love and women. For example: the first scene he shares with Beatrice; falling for Don Pedro, Claudio and Leonato's joke; talking to Beatrice after Hero has been denounced; the end of the play.

Romeo and Juliet

Foundation and Higher
Part (a)

- Exploration of Tybalt's reaction to Romeo being at the party. Use of pronouns, adjectives, verbs, repetition.

- Exploration of the disagreement between Lord Capulet and Tybalt, including Capulet's attempts to mask conflict. Use of gentle language to persuade Tybalt to leave Romeo alone, changing to direct, aggressive language when this doesn't work and he feels challenged. Use of verbs, adjectives, insults, repetition, short sentences, imperatives, exclamation, rhetorical question, threats.

Part (b)

- Exploration of conflict at another point in the play. For example: the opening scene; the fight between Tybalt, Mercutio and Romeo; family conflict between Juliet and her parents; the way the final scene presents the consequences of conflict.

Twelfth Night

Foundation and Higher
Part (a)

- Exploration of how comedy is created through Sir Toby. Use of pause, stagecraft, exclamation, wordplay, vagueness.
- Exploration of how comedy is created through Olivia and the Clown. Use of simile, list, repetition, references to Sir Toby.

Part (b)

- Exploration of another point in the play that creates comedy. For example: the hatching of the joke against Malvolio; the effects of the joke upon Malvolio; Viola (acting as Cesario) meeting Olivia; Fabian and Sir Toby's joke on Viola/Cesario and Sir Andrew.

Julius Caesar

Foundation and Higher
Part (a)

- Exploration of how Brutus is presented as a political conspirator. Use of pronouns, exclamation, euphemism.
- Exploration of how Brutus's use of contrasting imagery shows his real nature. Use of simile, adverbs, repetition and butchery imagery.
- Exploration of how Brutus is shown to underestimate Mark Antony. Use of adverbs, metaphor, simile, imperatives.

Part (b)

- Exploration of how Brutus is presented at another point in the play. For example: the early scenes with Brutus and Cassius; speaking to Mark Antony after the murder of Julius Caesar; his speech to the plebeians; confronting Cassius about taking bribes; his final scene before committing suicide.

Answers to Exam Practice Questions

The bullet points below are to help you understand the sort of content that the examiner would be looking for in your exam answer. The examiner would then use the mark scheme to work out how skilled you have been in your exploration and analysis of the text. Remember, the examiner will be expecting you to relate your ideas to the text's social, historical or cultural context.

Pride and Prejudice

Foundation and Higher

- Exploration of how Mr Bennet treats his wife and daughters, and the different effects this has on the family.
- Exploration of the ways in which he creates humour and social observation.
- Exploration of how Mr Bennet fits into the social and historical context of the time, such as attitudes towards women and class, and ineffectual parenting of the middle classes.

Wuthering Heights

Foundation and Higher

- Exploration of characters that represent different classes, for example Mr Lockwood vs Nelly Dean, Edgar vs Heathcliff, Catherine vs Heathcliff.
- Exploration of Heathcliff's changing social status and the role of money in class.
- Exploration of how different characters' behaviour links to the cultural expectations of class at the time, for example Catherine's reaction to Heathcliff upon her return from Thrushcross Grange.

Great Expectations

Foundation and Higher

- Exploration of Estella at different points in her life, for example as a child, returning from the continent as a young woman, as a married woman.
- Exploration of her treatment of Pip at different points in the novel, and how she has been affected by Miss Havisham.
- Exploration of how Estella links to her social historical context, for example reflecting a life of culture and wealth, her feelings of superiority over Pip, conforming to expectations of women at the time.

The Withered Arm and Other Wessex Tales

Foundation and Higher

- Exploration of how Mr Stockdale changes during the short story.
- Exploration of how love, duty, conscience and morality affect Mr Stockdale's character.
- Exploration of how the attitudes and behaviour of this young, educated, religious man reflect the social, cultural and historical context of the story.

Animal Farm

Foundation and Higher

- Exploration of different hopes and dreams and what they represent. For example: the Beasts of England song and its link to freedom and equality; how the idea of the windmill and its benefits keeps the animals determined; the (afterlife) stories of Moses the raven being discouraged, and then later secretly encouraged, by the pigs.
- Exploration of how hopes and dreams drive revolution in the story, how they are then used to manipulate, and how they are ultimately shown to be futile.
- Exploration of how the uses of hopes and dreams in the novel link to its historical context, for example the failures of Communism, manipulation by the Church.

Accent – changes in pronunciation due to someone's background.

Adjective – a word that describes a noun.

Adverb – a word that describes a verb.

Allegory – a text with an underlying meaning or message.

Alliteration – repetition of a sound at the beginning of a series of words.

Allusion – a reference to something else.

Anaphora – repetition of a word or phrase at the beginning of successive lines or clauses.

Atmosphere – the feeling or mood of a piece of writing.

Characteristic – a distinguishing feature or quality.

Class – a group of people with a similar social and economic position.

Colloquial – informal language used in everyday conversation.

Colonialism – where one country takes control of another land, usually for economic gain or exploitation.

Comparison – making note of the similarities between two or more things.

Conflict – opposition or fight between ideas or people.

Conform – to follow accepted standards or rules.

Connective – a word or phrase used to show how a new sentence links to the previous one.

Contrast – making note of the differences between two or more things.

Conventional – something that follows expectations, or accepted standards and rules.

Corruption – dishonesty or illegal behaviour; literal or metaphorical rot and decay.

Couplet – two successive lines of verse, which often rhyme or have a similar rhythm.

Dialect – words that are specific to a group of people, due to age or location.

Dialogue – conversation between two people.

Domestic – linked to the home or family.

Dramatic monologue – a poem in the voice of someone who isn't the poet.

Empathy – showing sympathy or understanding of someone else's thoughts and feelings.

Enjambment – when a sentence runs across a line or stanza of poetry, undisturbed by punctuation.

Euphemism – a harmless word or phrase which substitutes one (with the same meaning) that is considered upsetting or offensive.

Expectation – belief in how people should behave; waiting for something.

Fantasy – imagination, unrestricted by fact.

Fate – the idea that things in our lives are pre-determined by some higher force.

Feminist – a believer in equal rights and respect for women.

Fictional – something invented by the imagination.

First person – a story where the narrator is involved and refers to their own experiences.

Gender – classification of male or female.

Gender roles – behaviour that is expected of one gender.

Hypocritical – a person who pretends to be the opposite of what they are, through behaviour or speech.

Iambic pentameter – a line of ten syllables in verse, alternating short and long sounds.

Imperative – an order.

Impertinent – being disrespectful or rude.

Indigenous – originating from a country or specific area.

Intensifier – a word that intensifies the meaning of the word it changes (such as 'very').

Ironic – words used to imply the opposite of what the speaker actually means.

Juxtaposition – placing contrasting words or phrases next to each other.

List – a sentence containing a series of items or ideas.

Metaphor – a descriptive comparison that claims to be true (rather than 'as' or 'like' in a simile).

Monotonous – something that is dull, due to a lack of variety.

Monosyllabic – words of one syllable.

Morality – behaviour that distinguishing between good and bad, or right and wrong.

Narrative form – the style and structure that is chosen in order to tell a story.

Naturalism – a type of writing that aims for detailed realism.

Non-standard English – words, expressions or pronunciation that are not considered formal and correct.

Noun – a word referring to a person, place or thing.

Parenthesis – extra information that is added to a passage, and marked off by brackets or dashes.

Pattern of three – three closely-related words or ideas that are put together for emphasis (also known as 'rule of three' or 'list of three').

Pejorative – words that are deliberately negative.

Personification – a description that gives human qualities to objects or ideas.

Plosive – a sound that creates a sudden release of air when pronounced (for example, 'b', 'c').

Possessive pronoun – a word that replaces a noun and suggests ownership (such as, my)

Post-colonial – the state of a land after colonialism has ended.

Prejudice – unfair or unreasonable dislike or favour.

Pronoun – a word that replaces a noun (such as 'he', 'it').

Propaganda – information presented in order to persuade people to think in a certain way.

Protagonist – the leading character in a play or story.

Reality – things that are real, rather than imagined.

Repetition – repeating things for emphasis.

Glossary of Key Words

Rhetorical question – a question used to make people think, rather than one that requires a specific answer.

Ritual – a ceremony; a regularly repeated action or behaviour.

Rural – to do with the countryside.

Satire – use of mockery to expose something bad or incompetent.

Senses – the use of sight, sound, smell, touch and taste.

Sibilance – repetition of 's' sounds for effect.

Simile – a descriptive comparison that uses 'like' or 'as'.

Social constraint – having to follow what is expected of you by society.

Social conventions – expectations of 'normal' behaviour in society.

Sonnet – a traditional form of love poetry, written in 14 lines, in iambic pentameter and with a clear rhyme scheme.

Stanza – a group of lines in poetry (like a verse in a song or a paragraph in prose).

Syllable – the single units of sound that make up a word.

Symbol – an image or object that represents something else or carries extra meaning.

Symbolise – to represent something or carry extra meaning.

Taboo – something that is restricted or prohibited due to 'normal' social conventions.

Third person – a story told by a narrator who is not part of the narrative.

Tradition – customs and beliefs passed down over several generations.

Unreliable narrative – a story told in the first-person where you cannot necessarily trust the view of the narrator.

Verb – a doing word.

Victorian values – beliefs linked to strictness and morality, relating to late 19th century England and often seeming harsh or old-fashioned.

Acknowledgements

p. 4, 5 From *Martyn Pig* by Kevin Brooks. Reprinted by permission of the publishers, Chicken House; p. 4, 5 From *Touching the Void* by Joe Simpson. Copyright © Joe Simpson 1989, published by Vintage Books. Reprinted by permission of The Random House Group Limited and HarperCollins Publishers Ltd.; p.4, 5 From *Under Milk Wood* by Dylan Thomas. Copyright © Dylan Thomas 1952, published by Orion. Reprinted by permission of David Higham Associates Limited and New Directions Publishing Corp; p.4, 5 FROM KINDERTRANSPORT by Diane Samuels. Copyright © Diane Samuels 1995, 1996, 2008. Reprinted by permission of the publishers, Nick Hern Books Ltd: www.nickhernbooks.co.uk; p. 7, 9, 82, 85 Extract from *The Woman in Black* by Susan Hill, published by Vintage. Copyright © Susan Hill, 1983. Reproduced by permission of Sheil Land Associates Ltd.; p. 11 From *An Inspector Calls* by J.B. Priestley (*An Inspector Calls and Other Plays* first published by William Heinemann 1948-1950, first published by Penguin Books 1969, Penguin Classics 2000.) Copyright © J.B. Priestley 1947. Reprinted by permission of United Agents; p. 16, 17, 19, 25, 82, 85 From *Of Mice and Men* by John Steinbeck (Penguin 2000). Copyright © John Steinbeck 1937, 1965. Reproduced by permission of Penguin Books Ltd.; p. 16, 17, 21, 26 From *Purple Hibiscus* by Chimamanda Ngozi Adichie. Reprinted by permission of HarperCollins Publishers Ltd. © 2003 Chimamanda Ngozi Adichie; p. 16, 17, 26, 82, 85 From *Mister Pip* by Lloyd Jones. Reproduced by permission of John Murray (Publishers) Ltd.; p. 16, 17, 19, 27 From *To Kill a Mockingbird* by Harper Lee, published by William Heinemann. Reprinted by permission of The Random House Group Limited; p. 16, 17, 28 Abridged from the book RABBIT-PROOF FENCE by Doris Pilkington. Copyright © 2002 by Doris Pilkington. Reprinted by permission of Miramax Books. All rights reserved; p. 30 From *Les Grands Seigneurs* by Dorothy Molloy, from *Hare Soup* (Faber, 2004), copyright © Dorothy Molloy 2004, reprinted by permission of the publishers, Faber & Faber Ltd.; p. 30, 32 From *Medusa* by Carol Ann Duffy, from *The World's Wife* (Picador, 2000), copyright © Carol Ann Duffy 2000, reprinted by permission of Pan Macmillan, London; p. 31, 37 From *Poppies* by Jane Weir, published by the Guardian Review July 2009, copyright © Jane Weir 2009, reprinted by permission of Templar Poetry; p. 32 From *The Clown Punk* by Simon Armitage, from *Tyrannosaurus Rex Versus the Corduroy Kid* (Faber, 2006), copyright © Simon Armitage 2006, reprinted by permission of Faber & Faber Ltd.; p. 32 From *The River God* by Stevie Smith, from *The Collected Poems of Stevie Smith*, © Stevie Smith 1972, reprinted with kind permission of the Estate of James MacGibbon; p.32 From *Singh Song!* By Daljit Nagra, from *Look We Have Coming to Dover* (Faber, 2007), copyright © Daljit Nagra 2007, reprinted by permission of Faber & Faber Ltd.; p. 33 From *Checking Out Me History* by John Agard, copyright © 1996 by John Agard, reproduced by kind permission of John Agard c/o Caroline Sheldon Literary Agency Limited; p. 33 From *Brendon Gallacher* by Jackie Kay, from *Darling: New and Selected Poems* (Bloodaxe Books, 2007), reprinted by permission of Bloodaxe Books; p. 33 From *Give* by Simon Armitage, from *The Dead Sea Poems* (Faber, 2006), copyright © Simon Armitage 1995, reprinted by permission of Faber & Faber Ltd.; p. 34 From *Below the Green Corrie* by Norman MacCaig, from *The Poems of Norman MacCaig*, edited by Ewen MacCaig (Polygon, 2005), reprinted by permission of Polygon, an imprint of Birlinn Ltd, www.birlinn.co.uk; p. 35 From *Hard Water* by Jean Sprackland, from *Hard Water* (Jonathan Cape, 2003), reprinted by permission of The Random House Group Limited; p. 35 From *Cold Knap Lake* by Gillian Clarke, from *Collected Poems* (Carcanet, 1997), reprinted by permission of Carcanet Press Ltd.; p. 35 From *Neighbours* by Gillian Clarke, from *Collected Poems* (Carcanet, 1997), reprinted by permission of Carcanet Press Ltd.; p. 36 From *Mametz Wood* by Owen Sheers, from *Skirrid Hill* (Seren, 2006), reprinted by permission of the author c/o Rogers Coleridge and White, 20 Powis Mews, London W11 1JN; p. 36 From *Hawk Roosting* by Ted Hughes from *Collected Poems* (Faber, 2003), copyright © The Estate of Ted Hughes 2003, reprinted by permission of Faber & Faber Ltd.; p.36 From *Belfast Confetti* by Ciaran Carson (The Gallery Press). By kind permission of The Gallery Press, Loughcrew, Oldcastle, County Meath, Ireland, from *Collected Poems* (2008); p. 37 From *At the Border, 1979* by Choman Hardi, from *Life for Us* (Bloodaxe Books, 2004), reprinted by permission of Bloodaxe Books; p. 37 From *Flag* by John Agard, from *Half-Caste and Other Poems* (Hodder Children's, 2004), copyright © John Agard 2004, reprinted by permission of Hodder Children's, an imprint of Hachette Children's Books, 338 Euston Road, London NW1 3BH; p. 37 From *next to of course god america i* by E.E. Cummings, copyright 1926, 1954, © 1991 by the Trustees for E.E. Cummings Trust. Copyright © 1985 by George James Firmage, from *Complete Poems 1904-1962* by E.E. Cummings, edited by George J. Firmage. Used by permission of Liveright Publishing Corporation; p. 38 From *Hour* by Carol Ann Duffy, from *Rapture* (Picador, 2005), copyright © Carol Ann Duffy 2000, reprinted by permission of Pan Macmillan, London; p. 38 From *In Paris with You* by James Fenton, from *New Selected Poems* (Penguin, 2006), copyright © James Fenton 2006. Reprinted by permission of United Agents on behalf of: James Fenton; p. 39 From *Praise Song for My Mother* by Grace Nichols, from *The Fat Black Woman's Poems* (Virago, 1984), reproduced with permission of Curtis Brown Group Ltd, London on behalf of Grace Nichols. Copyright © Grace Nichols 1984; p. 39 From *Harmonium* by Simon Armitage, © Simon Armitage 2009, reproduced by permission of David Godwin Associates Ltd.; p. 39 From *Brothers* by Andrew Forster, from *Fear of Thunder* (Flambard Press, 2007), reprinted by permission of the publisher; p. 42 *Hitcher* by Simon Armitage, from *Book of Matches* (Faber, 2001), copyright © Simon Armitage 2001, reprinted by permission of Faber & Faber Ltd.; p. 47 *Stealing* by Carol Ann Duffy, from *Selling Manhattan*, published by Anvil Press Poetry in 1987; p. 49 *Blessing* by Imtiaz Dharker, from *Postcards from god* (Bloodaxe Books, 1997), reprinted by permission of Bloodaxe Books; p. 65 From *Animal Farm* by George Orwell, published by Secker & Warburg. Reprinted by permission of The Random House Group Limited.